Let's face it: we're all admittedly WIPs (Works in Progress) so it's good to know that God is with us WIP (While in Process). Wouldn't we all love that moment of a big reveal of the finally-finished-every-detail-in-place-better-more-amazing YOU? And then get to kick back and enjoy our perfect life? As if.

Instead, kick back in your real life mess and enjoy this fun reminder that The Master Builder is constantly remaking us.

~Anita Renfroe
Comedian & author

Right now I'm in the middle of my own home renovation project and I can tell you, it feels like it would be so much easier to do a complete tear down than to try to salvage anything from this falling down, what I'll generously call, home. And I've been there in my own life—wondering if there is anything even worth hanging on to. What you need in the middle of any restoration is an eye for what to keep, and what to get rid of. In their book, *Fix-Her-Upper—Hope and Laughter Through a God-Renovated Life*, Beth and Rhonda guide you through your own DIY project with the tools you need: Hope with a giant bucket of grace. It's messy, but the results are worth it.

~Kathi Lipp
Best-selling author of The Husband Project and
Clutter Free

Looking for a dose of encouragement, laughter, and practical, biblical help for renewing your life? Don't miss *Fix-Her-Upper* by my friends Rhonda Rhea and Beth Duewel! You'll fall off your chair laughing while finding tips for a reno-job on your life that will bring fulfillment, positive change, and a different kind of joy—one focusing on looking to Him, not on trying to be more perfect!

~Carol Kent
National Speaker and Author
He Holds My Hand: Experiencing God's Presence
& Protection (Tyndale)

Out with the old. In with the new. It's the way of God's grace. I promise you'll laugh while you learn about the beauty of a renovated life.

~*Jill Savage*
Author of No More Perfect Moms and
No More Perfect Marriages

A little laughter goes a long way in recharging a ramshackled spirit. But when you add the powerful truth of the Word of God, you have the blueprints for life renewal on a whole new level. *Fix-Her-Upper* is the real deal.

~*Jennifer Kennedy Dean*
Author, speaker and executive director of
The Praying Life Foundation

Love, love, love this little book about renovation, inside and out. First, I love the hilarious home reno stories that would make Chip Gaines burst into tears. Then I love the sweet and funny life reno stories…especially the part about melting pants (ya just have to read it!). And lastly, I love the down-to-earth way Rhonda and Beth bring scriptural Truths to real life for us readers to experience our own faith reno when doubts have begun their relentless spiritual demolition and our foundation starts cracking and leaking. Who doesn't need a reno from time to time to shore up, fix up, and perk up her sagging interior and faded exterior? We all do. And *Fix-Her-Upper* is a great place to start!

~*Debora M. Coty*
Speaker, columnist, and award-winning author of 30
books including Too Blessed to be Stressed series

Talk about a powerful tool in your spiritual tool belt! *Fix-Her-Upper* is just that tool. It will lead you right to God's amazing grace. I LOVED it!

~*Vickie A. Davenport*
Christian Television Network's
KNLJ Station Manager

For all who love a good transformation story, *Fix-Her-Upper* tells the most important one of all—ours. If you're feeling rundown, overlooked, and in desperate need of someone to help you see your potential, my friends Beth and Rhonda have a message for you. With humor and disarming vulnerability, they share their stories of attempted life-renovations, while pointing to the Master Designer who can restore any life.

~Glynnis Whitwer
Author, Doing Busy Better
Exec Dir. of Communications, Proverbs 31 Ministries

Let's face it—sometimes we all need a little bit of fixer-upper-ing. Our hearts and minds get twisted up in all the stress and demands of life and we find ourselves weary and worn. Rhonda and Beth get it! And their new book, *Fix-Her-Upper: Hope and Laughter through a God-Renovated Life,* is a poignant reminder that we have a Master Designer ready to renovate and restore all the messy places in our lives.

~Teri Lynne Underwood
Author of Praying for Girls: Asking God for the Things They Need Most

If you're looking for a spiritual life makeover, authors Beth Duewel and Rhonda Rhea have just what you need. With their newest book, *Fix Her Upper,* they illustrate God's principles with real life anyone-can-do-this application. This is the resource we all need for renewal and restoration!

~Edie Melson,
award-winning blogger, author, and speaker
Director, Blue Ridge Mountains Christian Writers Conference

Does your soul need some refurbishing? Heart need a little restoration? For anyone who's ever felt a little broken, we have a God of grace who is faithful to fix. In *Fix-Her-Upper*, Rhonda and Beth will guide you along your personal renovation!

~Athena Dean Holtz
Publisher, radio personality, pastor's wife,
author of Full Circle: Coming Home to the
Faithfulness of God

Wow! Do we EVER grow out of the need for God's *Fix-Her-Upper* GRACE?! NEVER! My very favorite TV shows and magazines feature before and after shots of house and home improvements. I love to watch people roll away the "old" and celebrate the "new." And isn't it always fun to see what a little heartfelt and friendly DEMO DAY can do for a worn out woman? This new book by my friends Beth and Rhonda will be a fresh shot of life renovation for any woman who like me, is always up for some grace updates. You will love it from the very first page until the sweet REVEAL!

~Pat Layton
Author Life Unstuck (Baker-Revell)

Fix HER Upper

Fix **HER** Upper

Hope and Laughter Through a God-Renovated Life

Beth Duewel
and
Rhonda Rhea

Bold Vision Books
PO Box 2011
Friendswood, Texas 77549

Dedication

To our husbands, Jerry Duewel and Richie Rhea,
the two best people we've ever known.
You guys bring joy and order into our crazy lives.
And so much love.

Table of Contents

Acknowledgments

Again, sincere smooches of gratitude to our hubbies/supporters/ encouragers, Jerry Duewel and Richie Rhea. Without these two amazing people, there's no way we could've pulled this book together.

High-fiving thank you's to the rest of our fams as well. We so love and appreciate our children! Duewel gang (Brittany, John, Brooklyn and Josh) and Rhea gang (Andy, Amber, Asa, Jordan, Kaley, Allie, Derek, Emerson, Daniel and Olivia), we love you all dearly and are humbled by your selfless investments of prayer, encouragement and all the various levels of cheerleading.

Sending out robust thanks to Bold Vision Books, and to Karen Porter and George Porter, who can be professional and still actually "get us," and who remain ever-fervent in their call to go further in ministry. More thanks to Maddie Scott for the sweet cover design. What a sweet blessing to have editor-extraordinaire, Cynthia Ruchti, lend her expertise and her wonderful, creative touch to this project. Colossal thanks to Cynthia!

Heartfelt gratitude goes out to Christian Television Network's KNLJ in Jefferson City, Missouri, and especially General Manager, Vickie Davenport, for partnering in all kinds fun and ministry. We appreciate you so!

Much thanks as well to Rhonda's prayer team: Janet Bridgeforth, Tina Byus, Diane Campbell, Mary Clark, Theresa Easterday, Chris Hendrickson, Melinda Massey and Peanuts Rudolph. Oh, my friends! Those prayers!

More genuine thank you's to Beth's family, friends and prayer team: Freda Barnes, Charlene Arnold, Barbara Kline, Patsy Dole, Dana Shymske, and the many other friends who prayed us through this book.

We are so thankful for agent and friend, Pamela Harty, who shares our heart for ministry, and for the folks at The Knight Agency who support the process in all the deets.

Sending along a note of special thanks to Steve and Betty Rhoads right here, for helping us work out details for a week of manic writing. You two are so wonderful.

Huge appreciation goes out to the Advanced Writers and Speakers Association. We so value the shared knowledge, prayers, support, encouragement and counsel.

And to those who labor alongside Rhonda at *HomeLife* magazine, *Leading Hearts* magazine, *SBC Life*, Edie Melson's *The Write Conversation, MTL magazine, The Pathway*, the Missouri Baptist Convention's official news journal, and the many other print and online publications who graciously grant space for Rhonda's humor columns, thank you.

More head-bobs of thanks to our church families at Troy First Baptist Church and Ashland Grace Brethren Church for consistent prayers and all the best encouragement.

Our deepest debt of gratitude is ever reserved for the Restorer and Renovator of our souls. Without His grace, we'd simply have nothing to share, and no way to even share our nothing. Thank You,

O Lord, for the grand adventure of the renovation work You have done and are doing in us. And thank You for the honor of getting to write about it.

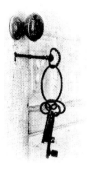

Introduction

We Are All Fix-Her-Uppers

Beth and Rhonda

All great designers have secrets—signature marks or special fingerprints that identify their personal touches. Granted, some designers leave more recognizable marks than others. Joanna Gaines, for instance. We love how she has made all kinds of marks with her love for the Lord and her passion for design. She's scattered shiplap like reno seeds across the vast acres of Waco, Texas.

We (Beth and Rhonda) may not be designers—yeah, not even a little—but we've both left a mark or two. Some are anything but pretty. We are confessed fix-her-uppers, and we've never hidden the fact that we're in need of big grace and extra big God-fixes.

Changes from the Uppest Direction

The good news? We have a big God who loves us enough to make those changes possible. We've experienced it! Seriously. With mercy and grace and tender love, He fixes our broken places in all the ways we long for. We love telling people that all of us can place our confidence in the perfect Designer, the one who created us for His redeemed purpose and plan. And we love teaching people how to experience this transformation for themselves. Paul clues us in to some of God's eternal design secrets: "For it is by grace you have been saved, through faith—and this is not from yourselves, it is a gift of God—not by works, so that no one can boast. For we are God's handiwork, created in Christ Jesus to do good works, which God prepared in advance for us to do" (Ephesians 2:8-10 NIV).

The divine Designer secret? If it's not grace—it's not God. These verses remind us that we are all fix-her-uppers in need of the redeeming power of Christ.

Along with this revelation comes another refreshing divine secret. We are God's handiwork. Each of us is a personal masterpiece fashioned by His hands. The Creator can only breathe life into His creation. Not death. You have life for a reason—His reason. And He desires to empower you to make your life count. So every time someone tells you that you're a "piece of work," you can happily nod. Yes! And it's a gift! A big gift of big grace.

Oh, that grace! Newness awaits us there. Joy. Purpose. Even a satisfied smile. Paul tells us in that Ephesians passage that once redeemed, we are instruments through which God trumpets His grace and glory. We've been repurposed.

Repurposing–Heavy on the "Purpose"

We can strip off those old layers and all our old ways of existing. We can live this life renovated. Together, we will find out in more detail just how to do that as we dig deep and focus on His power to renovate, His ability to restore, refresh, refurbish, revive, renew, and reclaim. We will discover that our Master Designer has His fingerprints all over our hearts.

Well, would you look at that! *We* bear God's signature mark!

It's our prayer that you, our reader-friend, will come alongside us in this renovation project. We're tickled to have some laughs with you. Even bigger though, we're praying that you will be all the more convinced that you are God's handiwork, that He delights in you, that He can fix your broken places, and that there are truths and principles in His Word that can help us all in this faith-reno process.

Each of the following chapters is written by one of us, with comments, "Added Accents of Colorful Hope," from the other, and with an extra verse, passage, or prayer included at the end of the chapter to help us "Fix Our Eyes on Him" and His truth. You can study the book from beginning to end and go through it at whatever pace fits your likes and your schedule. Or you can use each chapter as a day's devotion. The 28 chapters, plus an introduction and a conclusion, will give you a month of *Fix-Her-Upper* fun with some straight-from-the-Word fruit. Questions for personal reflection at the end of each chapter invite you to dig deeper in that "Bringing It Home" section. We encourage you to pick up a journal or notebook so you can write down your thoughts, answers, and Scriptures, cementing some of the principles and passages and taking them to heart in the most personal way. We warmly invite you, as well, to grab a group of girlfriends—any ol' time—for a fix-her-upper party. A leader's guide is also available. It includes instructions and helps for Bible study leaders/discussion group leaders. We would love to chime in on your discussions and studies! Feel free to tweet or Facebook message us. Tag us. We would love to connect.

So here we go, friends—ready to get renovated with you.

Part *One*

Renovate!

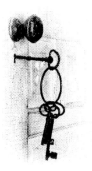

Chapter One

Do It Yourself Girl

Beth

I am a DIY adventurer. Not always the best aspect of my personality. My husband has learned to appreciate my frugality over the years though. And to overlook my flops.

Like the ornaments I made out of salt dough, which turned out looking like powder-covered cookies hanging low on a weighted Christmas tree. Jerry remarked when they started to mold in time-lapse fashion: "Why are there green cookies on the tree, honey?"

Poor guy. He was completely oblivious to the depths my creativity could teeter. I corrected, "They aren't cookies. They are *ornaments.*" In his defense, the mice clearly didn't "get" me either. But they did get three dozen packed and stored salt-dough ornaments to snack on all winter long.

However, DIY-adventurers like me remain optimistic despite adversity.

Once I decided to forfeit pre-pasted wallpaper. *Some bargains are bargains for a reason.* My enthusiasm was at an all-time high. I'd done decoupage. I could do paste. I slapped glue thick as Grandma's cupcake icing to the back of every eight-foot piece of paper. Apparently, Grandma needed more icing. A majority of the eight-foot edges curled up the very next day.

It's My Story and I'm Sticking to It

But, I had an idea. It was comparable to the childhood epiphany I'd had. It involved a paperclip, a string, and a light socket…but still. Did you know if you use superglue (and there are reasons a mom-on-a-mission should not get her impatient fingers on that stuff), and spill an ample amount on your fingers, and then if you quickly wipe it with the closest thing you might have (toilet paper), it can cause significant harm? A too-late look at the warning label revealed words like "toilet paper," "chemical reaction," "severe burns," "heat," "KEEP OUT OF REACH of children," and maybe even "KEEP OUT OF REACH *of mamas on a time crunch with a big project to complete!*" (mama-emphasis added). Again, true DIY-ers bandage all ten fingers and persevere.

You see, if there is potential in something, a do-it-yourself type girl desires to fix it. Now. She needs to fix it. She has to fix it.

Hence, my love for *Fixer Upper,* a TV show that screams out to our independent senses, "We can do anything on our own." The show resonates renovation bliss. One team comes in, another flows out. They make it look almost effortless, more like play than work, really, with Chip and Joanna Gaines completing house overhauls on their date nights.

A sledge hammer to a wall? No problem. A new sidewalk, terrace, or staircase? Even easier. So the thoughts pop into my head, "Hey, let's lay a wood floor the size of a basketball court on our own." Or "Install shiplap on our lunch hour." But once the tennis elbow hits (minus the tennis), my "team"—my honey and me—realize we might've had better luck whittling a miniature Mount Rushmore out of soap-on-a-rope. Nevertheless, it's the hope of what can be that keeps us colorblind to the gruesome, sweaty truth. Not all of us are as good at it as Chip and Joanna. And the even sweatier truth: Doing it all by yourself has its downside.

All by Myself!

Certain aspects of my independent nature have backfired. The sense that "I can do it myself" once kept me from recognizing this vital fact: I need God.

With a background in mental health, I understand the reasons for my self-reliant nature. My family of origin often pushed my buttons of fear, dependency, and unmet needs. My mistaken logic that said, "I don't need You, God," kept my young ego inflated like a balloon hovering over the land of "self-sustenance."

We're born with such inclinations. With my children, the battle started early. Tying a shoe had to be solo. Who cares if the bunny ears were loose and flopped to the floor? Coloring, playing, throwing cotton balls in the toilet just to watch them float like little white clouds—all independent measures to "go it alone." My son, so proud when he'd colored our hallway red and yellow, handed me his weapons and with a smile said, "All by myself, Mommy!"

Me? I demonstrated strong will and a positive drive to grow and learn. But then I grew up and heard myself telling my boyfriend (now husband), "Oh…maybe I'll get religion and go to church when I'm 30." I actually said that. I was stuck in the belief that God was someone or something you shop for while sauntering the aisles of a grocery store. You pull Him off the shelf when needed. Now I understand what the prophet Jeremiah meant when he wrote, "But these people have stubborn and rebellious hearts; they have turned aside and gone away" (Jeremiah 5:23). Our hearts blind us to the gruesome, sweaty truth: We can't go it alone.

The Real Fix

The day my mom died, I wanted to fix it. I had to fix it. I couldn't fix it! No amount of optimism or perseverance was going to be the quick fix or fill the hole the size of eternity that pierced my heart. A God-sized empty. The Bible reminds us, "He has made all things beautiful in its time. He has also set eternity in the human heart; yet no one can fathom what God has done from beginning to end" (Ecclesiastes 3:11 NIV). Only God could fill the whole of my empty and peel back my stubborn will. I had turned aside and gone down my own path. I'd tried "all by myself" to restore order and tidiness to my life. And failed.

Aesthetically everything appeared alright. Married only a year, I had a new job and a new place to stack duct-taped boxes that held high school year-books and my pink baby blanket. The splashes of color in my life were all a stark clash to the sterile white of my mom's hospital sheets. "She can hear you, you know. Even in a coma, she can hear you," the doctors tried to assure. I had no words. But God did. I picked up a Bible from the side table and let the pages fall in unfamiliar places. I didn't know the Bible. I didn't know God. Nor did I want to do it myself, alone, or my way…anymore. The list of things I'd thought would fix me through the years disintegrated while eternity lifted like the rich hues of a new day.

Fix-her-uppers really can have life renovated. It happened to me.

And although I still like to dabble in drywall putty, roll on some paint, or even carve leaves into a piece of sandstone just because I think I can, since that day, I recognize my daily dependence on Him. My life is put together with faith and grace. And sometimes a few coats of wallpaper paste.

Speaking of "put together," my honey and I have started our kitchen renovation. I love a good re-do, don't you? I'm just wondering where Jerry hid the superglue this time. Hmmm.

Added Accents of Colorful Hope from Rhonda

I'm celebrating the rebirth of Beth Duewel right now. I'm in awe of the beautiful way God so often uses the worst to bring out His best. He used even the grief over the death of her mom to launch Beth right into His kingdom. Glorious! I love how she is allowing the renovation to keep going in her life.

She's even keeping the renovation going at home. It would be entertaining to be a little mouse in that house. Not only could I watch all the beautiful slapstick comedy, but evidently I'd also be really well fed.

Fix Our Eyes on Him

"For it is by grace [God's remarkable compassion and favor drawing you to Christ] that you have been saved [actually delivered from judgment and given eternal life] through faith. And this [salvation] is not of yourselves [not through your own effort], but it is the [undeserved, gracious] gift of God; not as a result of [your] works [nor your attempts to keep the Law], so that no one will [be able to] boast or take credit in any way [for his salvation]. For we are His workmanship [His own master work, a work of art], created in Christ Jesus [reborn from above—spiritually transformed, renewed, ready to be used] for good works, which God prepared [for us] beforehand [taking paths which He set], so that we would walk in them [living the good life which He prearranged and made ready for us]"
(Ephesians 2:8-10 AMP).

Bringing It Home

Is there anything quite so sweet as remembering the day you gave your heart and life to Christ? Celebrate that day. If you know the date and haven't done so, write it in your Bible so you can remember and celebrate it often.

What details of your path to Christ do you now recognize as fine points of His plan to draw you to Himself? Pray a thanksgiving prayer to the God of grace who saved you.

Think about the "fixes" the Father has already brought about in your life. List a handful of the most dramatic ways you are different now than you were before and how life has changed. If you were a young child when you devoted your life to following Christ, think about how different your life is than it might've been.

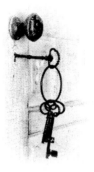

Chapter Two

Best Renos–Beyond a Doubt

Rhonda

Semi-accidental demolition. Sigh. During the years of raising all my kids, we often played the "We've-Got-Five-Kids" version of the game "Clue." It went something like this: Who did it? It was the toddler. In the family room. With a permanent marker. And there was never a whole lot of doubt there—but I never exactly felt like I won the game.

I'm not thrilled to tell you that Colonel Mustard also made an appearance or two. Once on my favorite comforter. (Can anyone tell me who in the world would need to eat mustard in my bed?) And red Kool-Aid made me fear Miss Scarlet greatly. Why couldn't someone just use a candlestick in the library and be done with it?

We held our things and furniture and carpets and walls pretty loosely in the days of raising all those kids, though it was still tough not to get just a little bent out of shape when yet another lamp would bite the dust. It still amazes me that no one knew who broke it or how it happened.

It wasn't only the kids doing the demolition either. One time a kitten clawed his way from floor to ceiling on my newly painted wall. He was halfway down again before I pulled him off. I'm pretty sure

I saw his life flash before my eyes. Is that a thing that can happen? Because I might've seen it nine times.

Without a Doubt

On the spiritual side of life, I have room for even fewer doubts than *who-done-it?* when the milk spilled or the refrigerator door was left open…the whole week of our family vacation. Believe it or not, doubt is much more destructive than five kids and a cat. It has a way of grabbing onto our joy and fruitfulness and clawing it up from floor to ceiling in the worst kind of demolition.

The enemy of our souls wields doubt. He's been effectively using it as a weapon since the fall of man. As a matter of fact, it was his weapon of choice in the initiation of the fall in the first place. "Now the serpent was the most cunning of all the wild animals that the LORD God had made. He said to the woman, "Did God really say, 'You can't eat from any tree in the garden'?" (Genesis 3:1, HCSB). Satan started the dialogue by casting doubt, then gradually worked his way down to overt denial of the truth and goodness of God. With a twist of God's words and a brazen lie, he told Eve, "No! You will not die" (vs. 4, HCSB).

The enemy still uses doubt as a weapon today. He knows if he can get us to waffle or waver in our trust in God, he can render us weak and worthless as far as accomplishing anything for the kingdom. Rather than winning kingdom victories, we essentially stay out of the devil's way and off his turf when we're tangled up in disbelief.

Got a Doubt? Get a Clue

Does your faith need a bit of a reno? Is doubt messing with what God wants to accomplish through you? Do you ever find yourself doubting that God is there? Or doubting that He will do what He said He will do? Or doubting that He sees you? Or doubting that He cares? Have you ever found yourself doubting His existence or His goodness or His power or His love? How can we renovate and renew that part of our heart and mind and soul? What do we do when there's a flash of doubt? Or nine?

Here's a clue. We grab onto faith, and we practice trust. That's it. And it works. Doubt will curl up and die as our faith and trust grow through embracing God's Word and letting it reveal more of who He is. Paul tells us in Romans 10:17, "So then faith comes by hearing, and hearing by the word of God" (NKJV).

The more we know Him—really know Him—the more our faith and trust grow. A small knowledge of God and a small understanding of Him equals a small faith. But knowing the truth about Him builds real, stable, super-sized faith with a supernatural foundation. Doubt dies right there. Here's where we as Jesus-followers truly get a better-than-the-game kind of clue. The big reveal? It's God. In your heart and mind. With His Word.

Faith That Leaves a Mark

If you struggle with doubt—or any time you're feeling a little weak or shaky in your faith—tighten the hinges on your faith through God's Word and its truth. Come to Him through His Word and in prayer in the most real and transparent way. The father in Mark 9 approached Jesus about healing his son in just that manner. Talk about a candid prayer. "I believe; help my unbelief!" (Mark 9:24). Any time we pray that prayer, He answers.

Make prayer and His Word part of your life every day. The combination will impact your faith as you see the proof of the power of your almighty God at work. It will leave a permanent mark on your life, my friends.

Which is, without any doubt, infinitely better than permanent marker on your curtains.

Added Accents of Colorful Hope from Beth

When in doubt, throw it out. Unless...you repurpose trash on purpose, then you keep it. Like that rusty bucket turned flower pot—a *rustoration* project, maybe? Its trash to treasure that you have to see to believe. And some renovations make an appearance in the most unlikely of places, don't they? For instance, a changed heart like mine. But aren't big projects just a grander showcase for God? It's so we look at the old and can only awe at the Creator of the new. A life resurrected from the decay of addiction or a heart healed from the punctures of pain and abuse. These treasures can only erase doubt and lend an air of truth to Rhonda's reminder: God loves permanent and on purpose.

Fix Our Eyes on Him

"Now Thomas, one of the Twelve, called the Twin, was not with them when Jesus came. So the other disciples told him, 'We have seen the Lord.' But he said to them, 'Unless I see in his hands the mark of the nails, and place my finger into the mark of the nails, and place my hand into his side, I will never believe.' Eight days later his disciples were inside again, and Thomas was with them. Although the doors were locked, Jesus came and stood among them and said, 'Peace be with you.' Then he said to Thomas, 'Put your finger here, and see my hands; and put out your hand and place it in my side. Do not disbelieve, but believe.' Thomas answered him, 'My Lord and my God!' Jesus said to him, 'Have you believed because you have seen me? Blessed are those who have not seen and yet have believed'" (John 20: 24-29).

Bringing It Home

Is there a doubt that has plagued you? Do you see it destroying your joy and your fruit? Write out a truth about God that nails your doubt to the wall. Make it a point to bask in that particular truth every day.

Make a concrete battle plan in other ways, too, to conquer doubt. Write out faith-building Scripture and put it somewhere you'll see often. Commit to memory those passages that destroy doubt and pump up faith.

What other strategies and tactics can you put into action in your plan to demolish doubt and build faith?

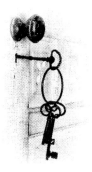

Chapter Three

Run-oh-vate

Beth

I know my strengths. I consider myself creative, adventurous and ready for new endeavors—unless those new tasks include either hanging Christmas lights or building our own home from scratch.

If you want to talk high frustration levels, though, Christmas lights max mine out. Is it just me, or does it seem like Christmas lights last exactly 365 days? On the 366th day we're forced to replace the ant-sized fuses. Which come in those ant-sized baggies. Of course, who really replaces a fuse for a string of lights that cost $1.00 during the after-Christmas clearance? Besides me, I mean.

Although fully aware of my ant-sized tolerance levels, my husband and I decided we were up for a larger adventure. We built our own home. If only it had been as stress-free as it always looks on TV.

You Might Run but You Can't Stomp

When you compare Christmas light frustration to home construction frustration, home construction takes top prize—times a zillion non-twinkling lights. Just when I thought I had a handle on balancing family, school, and work during our home build, the wrong color flooring was delivered and installed before we even knew it.

When we stopped by the project to check on all-things-home-construction, we found ourselves staring down at the perfectly-installed flooring. Perfectly installed. But entirely the wrong color. The mud my kids were stomping all over the new floor was actually closer to the right color than what we had there. Wrong color shingles for the roof. Wrong sized windows for the sunroom. Wrong this. Wrong that. It was like fixer upper gone all wrong.

To add to the stress from all the wrongness, a project timeline needs to be perfect, but the weather usually isn't. We were building in the middle of the deepest Ohio freeze. Out of toe-numbing desperation, we opted to rent an industrial torpedo heater. Thankfully, one cold afternoon, my brother-and sister-in-law offered to help with some of the construction details. When ice collected on our lashes, Freda and I defrosted by the torpedo's shooting flame. Until…"Freda, I think your pants are melting!"

Within a few seconds, the black vinyl covering from her exercise pants started to melt and disappear from the floor up. For real. She had no idea that the outer layer of her pants melted in time-lapse manner and left her standing in what looked like white cotton jammies. No question she was toasty warm. It's certain, home-building can ignite all kinds of heated frustration.

Stop, Drop and Run?

Frustration never seems to be in short supply. If your marriage can endure the countless stresses of life—complicated by a building project or not—you've outrun a few odds. Like any construction, a healthy marriage depends on a strong foundation. A God-foundation.

Good communication helps. A general contractor refers often to the blueprint. He or she is never far from the designer's and architect's plans. They stay in contact, as a married couple that values their relationship and are determined to discuss things well.

Relationships don't come in packages of ever-burning love and perfection. They spark, blow a fuse, and require daily upkeep. It's important to be committed to doing whatever it takes to resolve conflict before disagreements start to heat up. You know, that briefest pause before you're left standing in your white cotton jammies. The truth is that although I like to communicate—maybe even over-communicate—I've never been good at facing conflict and stress. Mostly I try to outrun it.

When we were expecting our first baby, I'll admit, I expected a lot. The books I read were not much help in that department. One of my faves was *What to Expect When You're Expecting.* I practically memorized all the pages of pregnant presumption. Then I asked Jerry to read the book, too. And I expected him to do it. You know, so we would highly anticipate and grossly overestimate the same things. But he didn't read it. Every day he'd come in the door from work to eye-contact and a list of loving assumptions like, "My face is totally glowing and I must have the crib and bassinet assembled tonight right after you demo the wall between our room and the baby's room (big breath here), pleeeeease." Did I not have 250 pages of practically-memorized "expectations" ready just for him? *With lots and lots of eye contact.*

A few weeks later, in breathless frustration, I ran out the door after a silly husband and wife argument. My mom used to ask me, "If your good sense runs out the door, will you follow it?" Yes. Yes, I will. I really don't remember the specifics or what struck the match and started the burn, but you can bet your sweaty estrogen there was some kind of discussion in which I "made plenty of eye contact." Misplaced hope and unreasonable must-haves had everything to do with it. The more I expected from my husband, the less I expected from God. Just the reverse of what I needed. It would be like an electrician expecting the painter to get the walls plumb and true. *Pleeeeease!*

Run to Him

Consider the woman plagued with bleeding for twelve years. Her ailment, according to Mosaic Law, made her ceremonially unclean. A social outcast, she faced wrong suffering. Wrong assumptions. Wrong diagnosis. Scripture tells us, "She spent all she had, yet instead of getting better she grew worse" (Mark 5:26). She had every real reason to be frustrated, and yet, she was a fix-her-upper gone right.

Like a broken window, others assumed her outside ailment revealed inside brokenness. They were all wrong. When she heard about a man who'd "healed many who had various diseases" (Mark 1:34), she ran to Capernaum. She put feet to her faith. The book of Matthew confirms her thoughts and expectations. "If I may but touch His garment, I shall be whole" (Matthew 9:21). The Greek word for whole is *holos*, which means "to be complete." She didn't need marriage, a career, every expectation met, or a clean bill of health to complete her. She needed His touch. And so do we.

Improperly placed expectation invites conflict, frustration, and heartbreak. We must have faith first. Faith is expectation and hope in its right place. And in right relationship to Jesus.

How much of Jesus is enough? "And behold a woman who suffered from a discharge of blood for twelve years came up behind him (Jesus) and touched the fringe of his garment" (Matt. 9:20).

One word from Jesus and all her expectations were exceeded, "Daughter, your faith has made you well; go in peace and be healed of your disease" (Mark 5:34). Jesus not only knew what she must-have for wholeness, He made her whole and called her His.

Jesus is the difference between being renovated and exasperated. Also, the difference between running and finding, hoping and having. God knows what we need and is clear about what He expects and what He knows is best for our hearts. "Jesus said unto him, Thou shalt love the Lord thy God with all thy heart, and with all thy soul, and with all thy mind" (Matthew 27:37 KJV). In essence, He was saying, "Let's start there. With the foundation of it all."

In the Long Run

The woman with the bleeding condition planted her feet on His firm foundation. She chose to be renovated and run to Jesus. To be run-oh-vated.

Knowing God is our only hope is not a new revelation. I'd have certainly saved myself—and Jerry—a ton of frustration, stress, and heartache if I had applied this precept in my heart sooner. *If I had touched the fringe of His garment.*

I want to be the wife of my husband's dreams. Of course, I also hope for all the aspects of a great marriage: good communication, forgiveness, and met expectations. The firm foundation is faith. God wants to renovate me and ignite my faith. What a respite for my tired heart. (Big breath here.) Sometimes even my tired feet.

Beth's words inspire me to seek more fringe. I want to reach for His robe first—before I run in all those other directions and toward all those other things. I love the concept of finding completeness in Him. When we become dedicated fringe-grabbers, we become wholly, completely, altogether all we're meant to be, in Him and for Him. A must have.

My goal is to stay on fire for Him in this poignant, touch-the-fringe way. On fire, but not torpedo-heater-on-fire. Because I have to tell you, the disappearing pants visual freaked me out.

Fix Our Eyes on Him

"Create in me a clean heart, O God, and renew a right spirit within me. Cast me not away from your presence, and take not your Holy Spirit from me. Restore to me the joy of your salvation, and uphold me with a willing spirit" (Psalm 51:10-12).

Bringing It Home

If we desire to know what we can expect from God, we need to go to His Word for revelation. Write out 2 Timothy 3:16. According to this verse, what can we expect from the Word of God?

Write down three Scripture passages that encourage you to run recklessly into the arms of God.

Have you ever seen God renovate someone who has been through a crisis or a devastating event? In what way did you see God rejuvenate that person's spirit?

Write out a specific prayer of renovation. Living in a state of renovation means giving mind, body, and spirit to God. Is there a specific area or areas you hope the Lord will renovate you? Include these things in your prayer.

Chapter Four

Inner Reno

Rhonda

It's not merely the houses. Could I just admit here that my eating habits could probably use some reno?

Eating on the healthier side of the food pyramid is a battle for me. My pyramid is much more…shall we say…*prismatic*. And probably at least a heptagonal prism at that.

I hear I'm not the only one. For those of us who struggle with food geometry, some days "diet victory" means we chewed the donut before swallowing it. (I would mention a "ring torus" here, but I'm really not that good at geometry.)

That battle to eat well? It's on the front lines. But related skirmishes break out in the conflict. I went to war this morning, for instance, with a pair of jeans. For the record, they started it.

When I finally conquered that top button, there was a great deal of satisfaction—maybe even a little gloating. It felt like victory. That is, it felt like victory until somewhere around lunchtime. That's when I realized that victory sometimes feels like getting slowly pinched in two.

I know there's a lot of war-talk here, but I do try to handle as much as possible through peaceful negotiations. So after lunch I took those jeans into my bedroom and had a long talk with them. I won't tell you everything that was said, but I will tell you I came out of the bedroom wearing sweatpants.

Yes, I do realize sweatpants are essentially the "I give up" of daywear. Sometimes, though, you have to choose your battles. Sometimes I choose breathing.

A Whole Different Battle

The spiritual battle against the flesh, however, is a different story. I'm not giving up on the battle for my heart. In Romans 13:12-14, Paul says, "The night is far gone; the day is at hand. So then let us cast off the works of darkness and put on the armor of light. Let us walk properly as in the daytime, not in orgies and drunkenness, not in sexual immorality and sensuality, not in quarreling and jealousy. But put on the Lord Jesus Christ, and make no provision for the flesh, to gratify its desires."

Sometimes what we wear is more important than breathing. Or eating. The Bible tells us to take off flesh and wear Jesus. Sometimes getting rid of all the fleshy works of darkness means we have to wake up to the fact that we're feeding it. We make provision for it. We follow it around or hang out where we know it might show up. We excuse it or hide it or rationalize it. But this passage tells us we're to stop providing for it. *Make no provision* for it. Don't feed it or water it or cultivate it. Take off the darkness and put on His light. We are called to take off the darkness of sinful living like so much cast-off, nasty-dirty laundry. And we are to put on Jesus. We're to be clothed with the very presence of Christ Himself. Putting on Christ begins that spiritual reno. He renovates life from the inside, out. He changes us from heart to mind and back.

Darkness to light. Like walking into a renovated building that had once been boarded up, but now boasts new windows with light streaming in.

Wearing His presence requires being controlled by His Spirit—letting Him rule our hearts and our minds so that it shows up in how we think and how we live. "For those who live according to the flesh set their minds on the things of the flesh, but those who live according to the Spirit set their minds on the things of the Spirit. For to set the mind on the flesh is death, but to set the mind on the Spirit is life and peace" (Romans 8:5-6).

Ah, life and peace. A peace that requires no negotiations. As we stop allowing our minds to go to those sinful places that result in sinful actions, and as we set our minds on Him, that peace just *is*.

Never Surrender, Ever Surrender

Never surrender in the battle against the flesh. Ever-surrender to the Lord Jesus. It's our submission to Him that brings real and lasting peace.

As far as the pinch-me-in-two jeans, I've tried to make peace there too, but we're still having some issues. So this message is for you, jeans: Don't you be giving me that innocent look. You know what you did.

Added Accents of Colorful Hope from Beth

I so agree with Rhonda. Inner reno's are a challenge. Allowing God to tweak my thinking, feeling, *and* doing is never easy. Then there is my saying. My tongue can be a super-sized sledge hammer with the potential to make every day a demo-day at the Duewel's. Words can build up or tear down. Like a wrecking ball, my words can fly without a thought to all of those hidden wires…feelings. My mouth—already swinging—has to stop and ask for forgiveness. Again. We are called to love before we speak, and speak only after we think.

Self-control restrains us to step away from the sledge hammer and pay attention. "We demolish arguments and every pretension that sets itself up against the knowledge of God, and we take captive every thought to make it obedient to Christ." (Cor.10:5 NIV.)

Fix Our Eyes on Him

A passage of surrender and a prayer of surrender

"Then David said to the Philistine, 'You come to me with a sword and with a spear and with a javelin, but I come to you in the name of the LORD of hosts, the God of the armies of Israel, whom you have defied. This day the LORD will deliver you into my hand… For the battle is the LORD's, and he will give you into our hand'" (1 Samuel 17:45-47).

Father, help us to surrender to You. From inside out, head to toe, heart and soul. Rule in us and around us. Empower us to stay ready for battle and to never give in when it comes to our flesh. And at the same time, remind us at every encounter that the battle is Yours. Just as it was with David and Goliath, all strength is Yours. All victory is Yours. All glory, Yours. Remind us in ways that give us confidence in our faith-walk, squelch fear and birth peace. Renovate us, we ask, in every way that really matters. In Jesus' name, amen.

Bringing It Home

As you read through this chapter, did you recognize anything you might be doing that could feed your flesh? Following it around? Hanging out where it might show up? Excusing, hiding, or rationalizing? If the Lord has shown you a sin you're "making provision for," and if you're really fed up with that darkness, draw a line in the sand. Work to rebuild good faith habits on a godly foundation. What concrete steps can you take today—right now—to stop feeding, giving in to and building on to sin?

Are there places you're allowing your mind to go, even if your body doesn't go along too? Put those places in the "darkness" category as well.

What are the practical ways you "put on" the Lord Jesus? And wear His presence? And remain controlled by His Spirit?

Part *Two*

Restore!

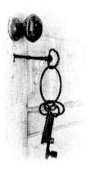

Chapter Five

Shabby Chic

Rhonda

It doesn't take long for anyone to figure out that I'm not the handy-dandiest DIY-er on the block. Not on any block. I do love shabby chic. Sadly, most of what I've tried on my own hasn't yet hit that shabby chic sweet spot. Most of my projects have ended up too heavy on the shabby. All too light on the chic. I had a dresser that looked distressed long before I distressed it. Before and after—both shabby. Not the good kind of distressed either. Just…distressed.

It's often in the middle of some of my most "distressing" projects that I find out what I'm really made of. I've had to make peace with the fact that I'm made mostly of shabby.

Making Peace with Who I Am–Also with the Dishwasher Door

While we're discovering who we are and what we're made of, forget all those personality tests. Never mind the character studies. Hold the temperament analysis. If you want insights into your own psyche, try the dishwasher. The dishwasher is actually quite the handy-dandy machine for revealing what you're really made of. All you have to do is follow these simple operating instructions: 1) Leave dishwasher door open. 2) Unwittingly apply shin forcefully to the side of the open door. 3) Repeat as needed. There's your temperament analysis.

A few years ago, for two or three weeks our dishwasher door wouldn't stay closed. Why weren't any of us DIY-ing *that?* By the end of those couple of weeks, I had taken a lot more personality tests than one personality can reasonably handle. Especially a sort of shabby one. It was also more than one person's shins could reasonably handle. My legs looked like a couple of old bananas.

Are those leopard print leggings?

No. No, they aren't. I wasn't wearing leggings.

I'm not sure why I didn't get better at maneuvering around that door. Or at least remembering it was there. Why didn't I learn to hurdle? I should've been Olympic-event-ready after the first few days. Finally, a strong leg survival instinct inspired us to get the door repaired. Until it was fixed, my family may have seen a little more of my "personality" than anyone would ever want.

What Are We Made Of?

We often find out what we're made of when we run into difficulties. Maybe even more so when we run into those difficulties really hard. How do we respond when we hit a surprise painful situation? Anger? Bitterness? Self-pity? Thinking life is unfair? Thinking God is unfair?

How we respond directly relates to the peace we will—or won't—experience in a painful situation. It's not so much a personality thing. It's not shabby versus chic. Peace depends on our own choices. In Colossians 3:15 Paul says, "And let the peace of the Messiah, to which you were also called in one body, control your hearts" (HCSB).

His instruction contains an important "let." We need to "let" His peace rule. Sometimes we let personality, or some other aspect of ourselves, control our hearts. There are times when we focus on the difficulty or the injustice and end up letting bitterness rule. Or we let negativity take over. Or sometimes we give in to fear and let it control how we live, think, and respond. Sometimes we let defeat or self-absorption rule. There are times we just plain surrender to sin and let it rule. Permitting sin to rule is distressing on every level, as is its impact on how we live. When we wallow in sin, we find less peace. Fewer victories. Smaller influence.

Those fleshly tendencies, the weakest, shabbiest parts of our spirit, certainly will control our hearts if we let them. The flesh wants control. And our flesh? Oh man. It has a strong survival instinct.

We Have a Referee

Our Father truly can renovate or reframe the way we see difficulties. And the way we respond to them. All the anger, bitterness, self-pity, and other knee-jerk reactions that bring out our fleshiest parts will only have control as we hand it over.

The Greek word translated "control" in the Colossians passage is a word that means to be a referee or director—like one who presides over an Olympic game. The indwelling presence of our Messiah and the peace that He gives will referee our every internal battle. Peace, my friends, wins the day at every point we will "let." It's like getting past everything shabby and gloriously grabbing onto the ultimate chic.

Is there anything else you're letting control your heart? Let His peace control instead. His control is the way to hurdle over any difficulty and win. Not just an Olympic win. A life win. Not merely refinishing the outside either, but experiencing a beautiful new peace on the inside. When we humbly surrender to His peace and surrender to His rule, we're able to be fruitful, joy-filled, thankful—spiritually chic! It's then we find we can successfully pass distressing trials with grace and come out the other side of those difficulties, those tests, stronger than ever.

Sure, even the personality tests.

Yes, even the dishwasher-door-to-the-shin personality tests. Though next time I hope we'll call a repair guy long before we reach the banana-legs stage.

Rhonda's right, we only need to bump into serious difficulty to find out what were truly made of. I confess that when the kids were tiny, I got tired of boiling pacifiers. I hated the thought of the germs, but I am a DIY-mom. I had a dishwasher and knew how to use it. A few cycles in, the pacifiers looked frothy, but I figured one or two licks would fix that. Then one day those pacifiers were gone. They must've catapulted off the top shelf and disintegrated in the bottom of the dishwasher. Like Rhonda's shins, some things are not dishwasher-safe.

It doesn't take much heat to dissolve away what I know to be right and true. My faith is sometimes only skin deep. Faith has to be a deeper, deliberate *knowing* to take the kind of heat life and the enemy tend to dish out. I may not be an expert on all things DIY, or even all things that "pacify," but I know when it comes to defeating flesh, the love of Christ and His Word is the only safe place to start.

Fix Our Eyes on Him

"But now thus says the Lord, he who created you, O Jacob, he who formed you, O Israel: 'Fear not, for I have redeemed you; I have called you by name, you are mine. When you pass through the waters, I will be with you; and through the rivers, they shall not overwhelm you; when you walk through fire you shall not be burned, and the flame shall not consume you. For I am the Lord your God, the Holy One of Israel, your Savior. I give Egypt as your ransom, Cush and Seba in exchange for you. Because you are precious in my eyes, and honored, and I love you. I give men in return for you, peoples in exchange for your life. Fear not, for I am with you,'" (Isaiah 43:1-5).

Bringing It Home

Any difficulties in your life producing responses like some of those listed? Anger? Bitterness? Self-pity? Thinking life is unfair? Thinking God is unfair?

Are there areas in your life in which you're allowing something else to take control—anything you're allowing to reign and rule? Do you ever let fear rule? Or selfishness? Grumbling? Negativity? A sin that's plaguing you? What game plan can you formulate today to take away the power you've given over to those things and let His peace rule instead?

In the space below, write Colossians 3:15 in your favorite Bible version and memorize it this week. Every time the Lord brings it to mind, let this verse remind you that He is the God of peace—that He loves you, that He is with you, and that He will give you peace if you will "let."

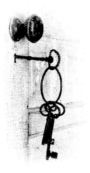

Chapter Six

Restoration Hardwire

Beth

Airport security checks? I'm not thrilled with those. Really, who is? Granted, they're vital, but going through security always makes me feel a bit uncomfortable. I'm wired like that, I guess. One reason it's awkward is that I'm constantly asking myself my own security questions. Like: *Did I take the metal nail file out of my purse?* On one flight, I checked for my nail file, only to be confused by the million cotton balls I discovered in my carryon. One cross look from security staff, and I knew I'd have to confess, "I have no idea how all those cotton balls got in there." Was it really necessary for me to confess that to the people in line with me?

We were headed to North Carolina to visit family. I was traveling with my dad, who'd been diagnosed with Alzheimer's. So, I'd checked and re-checked his carryon the night before—to avoid a security snag. He had evidentially re-re-checked more. Big snag.

There we stood in line at security, staring at an array of shiny objects he'd tucked neatly into his bag. Good gracious. I wasn't sure why he felt he needed the gold letter opener I gave him for Christmas. Or the giant nail clippers that looked hefty enough to trim an elephant's tusk. We were going to the Carolina's, not Africa.

Hardwire or Haywire?

I really wondered how many things could possibly go haywire in one simple security check. The X-ray revealed tiny screwdrivers, along with several other airline no-no's he'd brought along from his 25 years working at the *News Journal*. And wait! What's better than one bag of cotton balls? Two, of course.

As I readied all the other items to be shipped back home, I quickly discerned my dad wanted familiar items with him. Letter openers, screw drivers, and me. Even though I counted it a sweet gesture, I suppose it was good to know he was packing enough tools to break us out of security jail if we needed. Or at least tighten a few cell mate's glasses with those tiny screwdrivers to pass the time.

That's when I explained to the security staff about my father's recent diagnosis of Alzheimer's. His response sounded so believable, "Oh…don't listen to her—she's out of her silly mind!" His words were so convincing.

I couldn't fault my dad for any of it, of course. He was hardwired to be a hero—ready for anything. At home. At war. At work. Like aged wallpaper, if you checked under the existing surface, under all those crumbling memories, you'd find a man whose innermost nature is to save the day. Me? I might be more hardwired to fret. If you peeled back my layers, I'm worried you'll just discover more worry. But don't you worry.

Just when I thought we'd taken care of every concern in the security line, I stepped up for the scan and noticed a large sign that strongly encouraged empty pockets. Relief. I'd taken care of that. Then alarms blared. *Really?* We were escorted to another line and suddenly wands waved around my torso. My dad, the one who usually fixes problems like this, had on his high-volume father-type voice and thundered, "So. What. Did. You. Do?"

Huh?

Underwired

The woman with the wand gestured for backup and whispered, "Well, Ma'am, we think your bra is the problem." *Could this go anywhere good?* "The wire. But we're checking to confirm it."

My dad's hearing happened to be sharper than ever. His voice boomed, "What wire? You have a wire?"

What could I do but tell him my Vicky—as in Victoria's—secret. No longer a secret. To anyone.

Thank goodness my dad and I were also hardwired for laughter. We laughed until we cried. It was so strange to feel myself deflate into a tearful mess. Call me "out of my silly mind," but I was no longer in the mood to fly anywhere or visit anyone.

Once buckled and seated in the plane, my words tumbled out. "Dad, I'm sorry this is happening to you. I want to talk to you about us and some of our disagreements. I want to make it right between us before it's too late." I held his hand while he stared at the face of his watch. I had removed his watch batteries the week before. The concept of time and numbers had already escaped and become a huge source of frustration for him.

"Well, I think my watch has stopped," he said. "Honey, we don't have much time."

Hardwired for God

My father was right. Although I knew his comment was more about the stopped watch, God wanted me to understand something else. It was time. Time for me to let me go. My plans. My worries. My secrets. All of me. Our God wants to change us, to remake us. He loves us so much that He doesn't want to simply leave us as-is. He wants to restore us and reveal the beauty that lies beneath. But we must let go.

What we think about, worry about, and hold onto makes a difference. For me, worry is a thick layer of control in disguise. There is often an element of protection under every effort I make to manage life my way. Am I worried about uncontrolled circumstance, or do I trust God to exercise His control in my life? Do I trust God to lift parts of me—even through pain—to reveal the wholeness of Him?

It's amazing how painful a deep restorative change of heart can be. Uncomfortable. Restoration doesn't always feel like love. Soul-change often occurs through a goodbye, through an "oh-no!" and through letting go of ourselves and what we thought we white-knuckle needed.

It's no secret I'm hardwired to hang on when God clearly wants me to let go. I grasp unmet expectations, past mistakes, and bitter resentments. God wants to change me. He wants me to live as one who knows what it is to be restored. When I hold onto all of me, I hinder God's good purposes in my life. I must let *me* go. In the wise words of my dad, "Honey, we don't have much time."

Rewired for Saving

Mary was a woman who let go of herself. She anointed the head and feet of Jesus, and in the briefest moment invited repair. She understood restoration isn't as much the act of being redone, as it is the process of being undone. The practice of being relinquished and poured out.

"And while he [Jesus] was at Bethany in the house of Simon the leper, as he was reclining at table, a woman came with an alabaster flask of ointment of pure nard, very costly, and she broke the flask and poured it over his head" (Matthew 14:3).

Mary's perfume was priceless and could have changed her outside circumstance, but she wanted inside restoration. In laying aside her "me," Mary discovered the essence of what we are all wired to do: relinquish every worry, every circumstance, and every part of ourselves to God. I so admire her. She didn't waste any time. Mary refused to allow sin from the past or fretting about the future slow her down from finding God's good purpose in her life. She gripped something else. God's forgiveness and a broken flask.

Mary's story is told in all four of the Gospels, giving us a good look into a beautifully repaired soul. God wants to redeem us. He knows we deviate from His perfect standard of holiness, and that unless we completely empty of ourselves there's no room for Him. He knows sin covers us with grime and fades our beauty. His fix to our fade is forgiveness. His sacrifice to our sin is through His Son, Jesus Christ. His hope to our hopeless is the confidence we can have in a renovating love and the provision of a helper, "And hope does not put us to shame, because God's love has been poured into our hearts through the Holy Spirit who has been given to us." (Romans 5:5). When we invite His repair, we can trust His plan to be new in every way. Let's follow Mary's lead. We all have souls wired for sin, but hardwired for saving. Mary held nothing back, but poured everything out because, "Honey, we don't have much time."

My daddy, Glenn Williams, died a few years after that trip. And though he forgot my name, he never forgot how to love. Thanking God for time with him and all those hardwirings.

Added Accents of Colorful Hope from Rhonda

Haywired, highwired, hardwired, or hotwired. Even underwired. There's no wiring He can't fix. I needed this reminder from Beth to let go of "me," and to trust my Father. He is the God who loves to change us. To restore us. He doesn't simply leave us as-is, but He gives us a new hardwiring. *Lord, help us remember with every tick of the clock that Your love for us is immense and Your plan for us is good.*

And now can I admit how much I want to read this to my friend, Barb? Because, of course, she's *Barb-wired.*

Fix Our Eyes on Him

"She did what she could when she could—she pre-anointed my body for burial. And you can be sure wherever in the world the Message is preached, what she did is going to be talked about admiringly" (Mark 8-9 MSG).

Bringing It Home

Do you ever grip sins that slow you down and hinder God's good purposes for you? List some that tend to give you trouble. For each one, write down a verse that can remind you to let go of that sin and press into God's Word and His strength to change.

Restoration doesn't always feel like love. Soul change often occurs through a goodbye, through an "oh no," and through letting go of ourselves. Is there an area of your life in which you sense God repairing you?

If we read further in Mark 14, we find that the disciples were indignant about Mary's act because they saw it as wasteful. "Some of those present were saying indignantly to one another, 'Why this wast of perfume?'" (Mark 14:4). Is there some time, a talent or a tithe God may want you to pour out in generous worship to Him? Nothing is wasted. How will you respond?

Mark 14:6 says, "And Jesus says, 'She has done a beautiful thing to me.'" God views our worship as beautiful. Take a few moments to worship Him. Praise Him. Sing to Him.

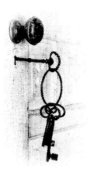

Chapter Seven

Restoring Your Smile

Rhonda

Isn't it funny that even though I'm a mess at DIY-ing, I spent several years working in a construction office? Yes, builders! I talked cabinets and sheetrock with home buyers. So a few years later when Richie and I were doing a walk-through inspection with a different builder for the home we were purchasing ourselves, I felt that instead of a walk-through, mine should be more of a strut-through. *Hey, I know what I'm doing here, guys.*

My builder buddies taught me how to check all the issues that tend to come up. I checked those issues but good, up one side and down the other. Like a pro. The hinges, the gutters—everything but the kitchen sink. No, hey wait. I checked that, too. Do you know how often that sink sprayer doesn't work? Not on my watch, buddy. I turned on that kitchen faucet, pulled out the sprayer hose, but accidentally grabbed it by the button. And oh, how it worked. It worked so well. I squirted myself full-on. Gusher—right smack in the face.

I can multi-task a lot of to-dos. But I'll tell you what I cannot multi-task, and that's looking like I have all the builder-savvy-swag in the county while simultaneously wiping at the mascara that's speedily made it all the way to my chin. All I could do was laugh.

Which made me look that much crazier, but no worries. That ship had already sailed.

The whole thing was so ridiculous it kept me smiling through the rest of the walk-through. Which turned out not to be a strut-through at all. It was more of a humbled grin-through. Also very well-hydrated.

A Grin-Through for Every Future

There's nothing wrong with multi-tasking or working to utilize our time well. Still, in the biggest picture, life is not all about utilizing our time. It's more about surrendering it. We're using time well when we're loving our Creator with all of it. And when we're remembering His love for us. Even in the most challenging moments, it's good to remember that His love is ever sure and steady.

Great strength comes from a keen awareness of His boundless love. There's great strength in loving Him with abandon. Difficulties can cause us to feel weak and fragile. They can make the future look dark and scary. But understanding His love for us and operating in loving surrender to Him gives a different outlook on the future. We can smile.

The virtuous woman described in Proverbs 31 is a compelling example: "Strength and dignity are her clothing, And she smiles at the future" (verse 25, NASB). This woman is strong—she "wears" that strength—and she smiles at what's ahead.

Resting in the love of God, relying on Him, strengthens us to the point we don't have to fear difficulties. "Praise the LORD! Blessed is the man who fears the LORD, who greatly delights in his commandments! He is not afraid of bad news; his heart is firm, trusting in the LORD. His heart is steady; he will not be afraid" (Psalm 112:1, 7-8).

Ah, there's that key to a sincere smile. A heart that's firmly, steadily trusting in the Lord doesn't fear. Peaceful rest is built into that trust, just like rebar that is not visible, but lends immeasurable strength to a concrete slab.

My grandmother once had an electric blanket that had to be from the pit of the hottest parts of the darkest abyss. But she paid good money for it, so we were going to use that thing or die. I worried it might be both. We didn't need a nightlight at Grandma's. The little sparks from that blanket did the trick. Never mind the flames. Just pat those puppies out, turn over and go back to sleep.

Every once in a while, life can feel a little like my grandma's blanket. When you think life is comfy and warm, you feel flames instead. It can be difficult to smile—faith-filled and hope-anchored—when you're trying to squelch little flames. Sometimes you may even wonder if God sees your discomfort or if He cares.

He Sees, He Cares, He Loves, He's Here

Could I encourage you in those moments of doubt to hold onto a confident knowledge that not only does He see your pain, and not only does He care about you and about your hurt, but He's right there with you? He's with you in every distress.

"Where shall I go from your Spirit? Or where shall I flee from your presence? If I ascend to heaven, you are there! If I make my bed in Sheol, you are there! If I take the wings of the morning and dwell in the uttermost parts of the sea, even there your hand shall lead me, and your right hand shall hold me. If I say, 'Surely the darkness shall cover me, and the light about me be night,' even the darkness is not dark to you; the night is bright as the day, for darkness is as light with you" (Psalm 139: 7-12).

Even when you feel blanketed in everything heavy, dark and uncomfortable, you can know that He sees right out the other side of that darkness. And through it all, He is with you. He lives right inside you.

The Holy Spirit of God has been with you every moment of every day since the instant you surrendered your life to Christ. Jesus said, "And I will ask the Father, and he will give you another Helper, to be with you forever, even the Spirit of truth, whom the world cannot receive, because it neither sees him nor knows him. You know him, for he dwells with you and will be in you." (John 14:16-17).

Our Helper/Comforter. His forever presence! Now there's a Comforter we can lean on for the coziest sense of wellbeing, even when the heat is on. Recognize His presence and you will find sweet rest and beautiful restoration every time.

I'd rather spend my time relying and resting in the Lord, not fearing and fretting over difficulties. It's true, I can always find a restored smile there. I can lie down at night. I can sleep peacefully.

"In peace I will both lie down and sleep, for You, Lord, alone make me dwell in safety and confident trust" (Psalm 4:8 AMP).

Sleep with a smile. Likely no mascara, but that's okay.

Added Accents of Colorful Hope from Beth

The word "restore" certainly sparks a memory for me. When Jerry and I were first married, I restored a pie-safe a flood had all but destroyed. I spent months in our cold garage with a heat gun. Talk about sparks! You'd be surprised what a heat gun can do when you add a little paint and the peach fuzz on your arms. Multiple burnt spots in the wood and two broken pieces of antique glass left me with nothing to smile about by the end of the project. I didn't let a few imperfections stop me, though. Or a few fuzz-less knuckles. It even reminded me a little of myself. Salvaged from ruin. Imperfect. Restored. So on second thought, there is something to smile about there. Still smiling.

Fix Our Eyes on Him

"Behold, he who keeps Israel will neither slumber nor sleep. The Lord is your keeper; the Lord is your shade on your right hand. The sun shall not strike you by day, nor the moon by night. The Lord will keep you from all evil; he will keep your life. The Lord will keep your going out and your coming in from this time forth and forevermore" (Psalm 121:4-8).

Bringing It Home

Are you ever tempted to forget about His intense and steady love for you because of a difficulty you experience? What are some practical ways you can renew your awareness of His great love? Write some of your favorite verses about His love in your journal.

Is John 3:16 in your list? In light of this verse, can you imagine that there would ever be anything that you really need that the Lord would withhold from you? Look at the last part of Psalm 84:11 and jot it in your journal if it's not there already: "No good thing does he withhold from those who walk uprightly."

List some of the strengths you see in the woman described in Proverbs 31:10-31. What do you see as her greatest strength? Which strength do you think God counts as most admirable?

How does loving the Lord and recognizing His presence change how you see difficulties?

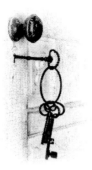

Chapter Eight

Is There a Blueprint for This?

Beth

I bit my lip hard as I made eye contact with my daughter's reflection in the beauty shop mirror. Brittany's furrowed brow matched mine while my mother-instincts needled me. My plan to help her was failing. Miserably.

Granted, I had no strategy to follow. I mean, is there a blueprint for this sort of thing, some answers to my many questions since hearing the words five months earlier, "I'm so sorry, but your daughter has a brain tumor"?

I was flying blind on this one. And so was the sweet lady helping us as she fished deep into the cardboard corners of a gigantic box. Her determined grimace told us she wasn't about to be detoured by my disappointment. *Oh thank goodness.*

Because it's true. Moms on a mission can be hard to please. We can't help it. It's not as if we're trying to be difficult. Mommy-fix-it-ness just oozes out of us like the urge to slick down a cowlick. We've got to slick, kiss, or fix something. We love *that* much! *Love* was the reason I'd told Brittany, "Don't worry. I have a great idea!" So, I called the beauty shop to see if there was something they could do. They said they knew a lady. Believe me, I had no clue my "great idea" would land us in a back room with damp, wilting boxes and tons of tangled tresses.

But a verse in Proverbs encouraged me as I watched the kind woman place yet, another...um...untidy tuft of "something" onto my daughter's head. "Trust in the Lord with all your heart. And do not lean on your own understanding. In all your ways acknowledge him, and he will make straight your paths" (Proverbs 3:5-6 NASB).

Trusting my own plan, my own life blueprint, or my own understanding was like trying to build a house framed with paper walls.

Blueprints Can Be Difficult to Read

The day before, more of my paper walls shredded like confetti when Brittany hopped into the car after school. "I hate wearing hats!" Her tears escaped with the groan of the passenger door.

She had returned to school two days earlier, following her surgery and illness.

"Mom, a boy pulled off my hat...while I was walking to class. He pulled it off and threw it down the hall!" Her ball cap had been her chosen protection from questions and stares.

"What are we going to do, Mom?"

All I could say was, "Pray." How I hurt for her. The incident was enough to send this high-drama-mama searching for an answer for her in the back room of a beauty salon. But a stolen hat and a traumatizing reveal seemed small in light of the miracle of "still alive." God was surely building a stronger faith-foundation for our entire family, not from paper, but from these new painful pieces of our lives.

I remembered the words from one of her doctors three weeks earlier. He'd questioned my mom-sense. "If it were my daughter, I wouldn't let her go back to school. What grade is she in...eighth?" He pointed out that people at school would notice that Brittany looked different than before her illness. And students can be mean. He shared more—most of it even more pointed and harsh.

"Mom, I want to see my friends," she'd said. "There are only a few weeks left before the end of the year. And my friends will love me for who I am inside. Anyway, we already prayed about this." Brittany spoke calmly, matter-of-factly, as if she hadn't a single worry. Then she laid down to sleep.

Good gracious, she was right. It was as simple as that.

Trading Paper for Perfect

Brittany displayed a simple trust in God's restorative plan for his children. And really how can one be restored if not broken, worn out, out of answers, and exhausted first? Could it be that God was using the painful pieces to build a wall of understanding that would hold us up? All along we'd prayed God would restore Brittany's health, completely. Fix it. On the way home from the doctor's appointment though, I wondered if He had in mind to do so much more.

Like when Jesus fed the five thousand. The true miracle was not merely the provision—even though God's supernatural provision for the hungry people was miraculous. Jesus wanted to do more. He wanted to restore!

Scripture reminds us the people stood all day listening to Jesus' teachings. They were hungry and tired. Jesus already knew what he was going to do, and a boy showed up with what amounted to a child's sack lunch. One of His disciples said to Jesus, "'There is a boy here who has five barley loaves and two fish, but what are they for so many?' Jesus said, 'Have the people sit down.' Now there was much grass in the place. So the men sat down, about five thousand in number" (John 6:9-10).

Why would Scripture point out such a trivial detail as "there was much grass in the place?" Maybe it's the same reason God wants us to know this amazing truth. "And when they had eaten their fill, he told his disciples, 'Gather up the leftover fragments, that nothing may be lost'" (John 12:13).

It wouldn't have been a stretch for Jesus to whip up a few more fragments. And it wouldn't have been a stretch for God to make the hard days easy for my daughter. But He generously allows our pain to expose something more. More joy. More faith. More beauty.

Beauty is Pain

But what a comfort to this mamma's heart. God does not waste anything.

He does not waste pain. He does not waste our mistakes. *Oh, thank goodness.* He does not waste the fragments in a difficult marriage, a stressful career, a difficult loss, or in any bad moment of any bad day. My friends, He goes after breadcrumbs. He loves more than enough to provide more than enough! He loves more than enough to restore over and above. The foundations laid by Him are strong. His blueprint is perfect.

Even that day in the back room of the beauty salon, we had glimpses of His perfect plan. Neither Brittany nor I could hold back sincere but uneasy smiles as the kind lady gave one last try at fitting Brittany with the perfect contents from the perfect wilted box.

What was that thing the woman put on Brittany's head? So far from ideal. So, so far.

We were both relieved that we made it out the door before exploding into laughter. That's when we knew. There would be no more hats. Brittany decided she would live with the remaining fragments of her hair, knowing God was slowly but beautifully restoring.

God. Does. Not. Waste. A. Thing.

Added Accents of Colorful Hope from Rhonda

There's nothing that pains our mommy-hearts like seeing our children hurting. There's not much that can bring joy to that same heart, either, like seeing our children grow in character and wisdom. I'm sad my friend Beth had to experience this. And I'm happy my friend Beth got to experience this. What a beautiful way our God has of bringing the awesome from the awful, bringing the most delight from what we were sure would be the most devastating. It's beautiful to remember as well that we have a God who feels our pain infinitely more than we feel our children's. Praise to God, who doesn't waste a thing.

Fix Our Eyes on Him:

"And after you have suffered a little while, the God of all grace, who has called you to his eternal glory in Christ, will himself restore, confirm, strengthen, and establish you" (1 Peter 5:10).

Bringing It Home

How do you see your heavenly Father using a difficulty to build your faith? Do you think it could turn into a faith-builder for your family or friends, as well?

It's perfectly right for us to pray and ask God to work, or heal, or "fix" when we're in the middle of something hard or trying or heartbreaking. Are you willing and trusting in the midst of it all to submit to His plan? Can you imagine Him doing "so much more"?

Have you ever experienced a pain, then see the Lord do His "something more"? Have you experienced difficulty you've found yourself later praising God for?

What are some "breadcrumbs" the Lord might be gathering in your life?

Part *Three*

Refresh!

Chapter Nine

Fresh Sense

Beth

I've always wanted to be brave and fearless. Spontaneous, with cares cast to the wind. I'm none of those. Except maybe spontaneous.

My spontaneity sparked as North Market Spices threw wide its doors, inviting a friend and me in like a chai latte invites whipped cream. Shelves bulged with jars hosting unusual concoctions—Mexican Hot-Cocoa, Basil Mania, and Vanilla Bean Blast. It was Christmas in March for the nose.

The first jar labeled with the word Chai practically jumped off the shelf into my hands. Unfortunately, my friend was busy and didn't catch wind of what I was about to do.

(Insert long sniff here). Now wait for it. Wait for it…

Ahhh…smells like Chai. And a cozy fire. It took me a second to realize it wasn't actually a cozy fire. Just *fire!* My nostril hairs practically sizzled while I strained to read the label through my tear-filled eyes: Chai-Habanero! *What?* The label was bold. The label was even at nose level. The label was still not enough to keep me from burning up a few brain cells.

Patsy has been my friend for many years, so she's used to this sort of episode. "What on earth possessed you to sniff something that said 'habanero'?"

Two coughs and a lengthy moan were all I could muster in response.

"Are you okay? Are you going to cry?" Her questions offered some comfort, even though I knew she was probably thinking, *What kind of public spectacle is she going to make of herself this time?"* She didn't think it out loud. And thankfully, best friends often have a way of shining a better, less offensive light on these things.

Where is a vendor selling Kleenex when you need one? I managed to find a paper towel at a nearby pastry shop. Paper towel was close enough. In fact, it seemed a better fit.

How Did I Miss that Sign?

I was still toweling off when Patsy led me back to a palm-sized piece of paper: "SNIFF ALERT!" *Huh?* I'll admit, even 72 point font stays blurry through that kind of teary squint. I mean, has the owner considered a flashing neon sign? You know, for urge-driven customers like me? Or the one urge-driven customer like me? Or maybe just me?

Unfortunately, it often takes something like a spark of habanero to capture my attention spiritually. Prone to wander through fields of Chai-laden comfort, my spiritual disciplines can become stale, and sometimes I slack.

First Peter 5:8-9 NIV reminds us to, "Be alert and of sober mind. Your enemy the devil prowls around like a roaring lion looking for someone to devour." Granted, not a spa-type message. But it's way too easy to become spiritually sluggish, or even so busy we lose our "sober" mind.

And take a whiff of that word: *devour*. "Devour" (*v*)-to eat (food or prey), hungrily or quickly. That type of pursuit and that kind of appetite requires prudence in the ways in which we renew ourselves through Christ each day. Breathing Him in can completely replenish. What are additional ways we can stay spiritually alert?

Breathe in Deeply

Waking up with a big breath of God's Word helps jumpstart a fresher, less painful day, for sure. But if I rush out the door in the morning while I wrestle my hair into a black rubber band, I can still try to follow the yellow lines to work by incorporating unhurried praise. Praise music, a praise-filled verse, and praise-filled moments help pace my breathing with His.

Ann Voskamp cites her praises in her book, *One Thousand Gifts* (Zondervan, 2011), her cadence simple and the rhythm slow. "I begin the list. Not of gifts I want but of gifts I already have. 1. Morning shadows across old wood floors. 2. Jam piled high on the toast. 3. Cry of blue jay from high in the spruce."

My list as I remember to "breathe" is less romantic, but still focused and natural. 1. Morning tea overflowing onto floor. 2. Lights from a school bus flashing. 3. God's listening ear through the fog. Praise-shaking complacency awakens my soul like a hand awakens after it's fallen asleep. Capturing my mind, keeping me breathing.

Breathe Out Intently

Another way to invite God to renew me spiritually is to make certain I have significant accountability. By having an accountability partner for more than fifteen years, renewal has remained an important part of my spiritual attentiveness.

In addition to another voice (besides the distracted one in our head), a friend can wake us up to thoughts like, "Step away from that habanero!"

Accountability can serve not only as an alarm, but also as a voice of encouragement and challenge. God hears me whispering inside, *A little help here, Lord*, and He sends a friend. Can't we all sometimes use a nudge to try a new ministry, go on a mission trip, or memorize new Scripture? Sometimes it's as simple as pointing out a sign we missed, in hopes of avoiding a painful consequence. A friend who can direct us to lean into the Holy Spirit's leading is a much-needed breath of fresh air. Since it's easy to be nose-blind to our own spiritual staleness, staying answerable to someone else helps us stay fresh and Christ-centered. Spiritual lethargy can catch us off-guard. Take it from one who "nose." An extra set of eyes, ears, and knees can be very effective in revamping spiritual fervor. It makes sense.

Just Breathe

Although these alerts encourage me to wake up and smell God's goodness, if I mess up, I can still breathe (or sniff), a sigh of relief.

Thank goodness. The deceiver may pursue, but God pursues *more*. I can rest. Rest in a God who never sleeps. Always forgives. Always refreshes. Always renews and breathes life into my soul. Ahhhh.

"The Spirit of God has made me, and the breath of the Almighty gives me life" (Job 33:4). So now that I've come to my fire-charged senses, I might even try shopping at that spice store once again.

I *will*, however, pack a few extra Kleenex.

Added Accents of Colorful Hope from Rhonda

Oh be careful, little nose, what you sniff. Then again, if a whiff of something fiery—or staying consistent in His Word, or connecting with a godly friend—if any of that will help in staying on fire for Christ, I'm in. *The Message* paraphrases Romans 12:11-12 this way: "Don't burn out; keep yourselves fueled and aflame. Be alert servants of the Master, cheerfully expectant. Don't quit in hard times; pray all the harder."

Look, Beth. "Fueled and aflame." We should all be as habanero-ey as you!

Fix Our Eyes on Him

"Take your everyday, ordinary life—your sleeping, eating, going-to-work, and walking-around life— and place it before God as an offering. Embracing what God does for you is the best thing you can do for him. Don't become so well-adjusted to your culture that you fit into it without thinking. Instead, fix your attention on God. You'll be changed from the inside out" (Romans 12:1-2 MSG).

Bringing It Home

Renewal can be a lengthy process. But a one-day-at-a-time approach may help create the fresh start needed. Choose one intentional step toward renewing your spirit and then apply practically to your day. Can you categorize it as spiritually "breathing"?

Write out 1 Peter 5:8-9 and take some time to commit it to memory.

Make a list of practical action steps you can do to help maintain a God focus and keep your mind "sober."

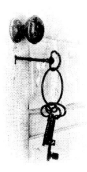

Chapter Ten

Follow the Instructions

Rhonda

Becoming efficient as a "fixer" and learning how to be extremely "upper" about it—shouldn't that be as easy as finding the right directions? Then again, I have trouble following a recipe. On a box.

As a matter of fact, it's really funny when I read the directions on the brownie mix box, and then throw the box away. Like I somehow think I *won't* have to dig it out of the trash five minutes later. Or dig it out eight more times after that.

Sometimes I totally forget how to boil brownies.

Not that there's a lot of ADD at work here or anything, but I was looking up the symptoms for ADD the other day and ended up watching puppy videos on Facebook for 45 minutes.

Take one large portion of forgetfulness. Fold in equal measurements of all the attention deficits. Then add a generous sprinkling of puppies. What do you get? Well it's not brownies, I'll tell you that right now.

One time I was in a meeting with an editor and suddenly noticed that when I polished my nails, I missed one. Nine painted nails. What? I forgot how many fingers I have? So I was supposed to convince an editor that I could responsibly finish an entire book when I couldn't even manage to polish all ten fingernails. *Focus, girl.*

How About a Personal Meeting with the Father?

My focus will probably always come and go. And then probably go. But I don't want to be forgetful, distracted, or careless when it comes to God's message for me. In Christian circles, we speak often about reading God's Word. Why do you suppose we make such a big deal about the Bible?

Probably the biggest reason is that whatever measure of attention we give the Word of God, by that measure we'll grow. No attention, no growth. Simply reading the Bible is not really the goal. It's not about ritual. The goal is to *know God*. To open His Book—His personal message to us—and to meet with Him there. The Father's is a message that makes sense of life. A message that grows us. And even more, a message that completes us.

We looked at part of this passage earlier. Paul wrote that "All Scripture is inspired by God and is profitable for teaching, for rebuking, for correcting, for training in righteousness." He also wrote about what all the training is for: "So that the man of God may be complete, equipped for every good work" (2 Timothy 3:16-17 HCSB).

Any time we're feeling disconnected or directionless— "incomplete"—it's important to examine how focused we are on meeting with the Father through His Word. It's time to dig those instructions back out. The word "complete" in 2 Timothy 3:17 is from the Greek word *artios*. It's a math concept that implies that nothing else needs to be added to make it whole. All-inclusively perfectly polished.

If your desire is to be "artios," start with His Word. When you boil it all down, isn't that desire to be whole—to have a deep and meaningful relationship with our Creator—what we all want in life? It's exactly what we were made for. Without that complete connection, life will always seem a bit…off. Not quite right.

May we wisely trade that "not-quite-right-ness" for the completeness we find in our Creator and in connecting with Him through His Word. Completeness. And answers to the questions we truly need to have answered.

What do we mean by "Finding Answers"?

There are a lot of reasons I'll never be on *Jeopardy*. One big one is that I can very reasonably imagine Alex Trebek saying something like, "Please remember to phrase all your ignorance in the form of a question." *Um, I'll take "No Way I'll Ever Get Any of These Right" for 200 please, Alex."*

What if the question that's the answer isn't my answer? What if my question is really a question? Because I don't *know* the answer to the question—or the question to the answer? See, I'm completely confused, and we haven't even gotten to any real questions.

The good news is that even though I may not know the answers to all the questions—or the questions to all the answers—I do know where to find what I really need to know to determine my way in life. I'm pressing the button here. Anytime we need light for life's path, God's Word is the answer. "I do not turn aside from your rules, for you have taught me. How sweet are your words to my taste, sweeter than honey to my mouth! Through your precepts I get understanding; therefore I hate every false way. Your word is a lamp to my feet and a light to my path" (Psalm 119:102-105).

People often talk about the difficulty they have understanding God's Word. But the Lord honors our seeking. I love Proverbs 8:9-11. It's about the One who gives us clarity. "My words are plain to anyone with understanding, clear to those with knowledge. Choose my instruction rather than silver, and knowledge rather than pure gold. For wisdom is far more valuable than rubies. Nothing you desire can compare with it" (NLT). The Father gives wisdom and understanding as we seek Him. And it's more valuable than anything material.

Psalm 119:36-37 (HCSB) backs that up: "Turn my heart to Your decrees and not to material gain. Turn my eyes from looking at what is worthless; give me life in your ways." Material things—stuff— are like life-points never redeemed. But the way of the Lord? It *is* life! Just a few verses earlier, we're reminded again who gives us the ability to understand these truths. "I pursue the way of Your commands, for You broaden my understanding" (Psalm 119:32 HCSB).

In Hot Pursuit

As we "pursue" as the psalmist did, the Lord continues to make His truths clear. Pursue understanding, and He will give real life. Ask the Lord to open your eyes to His treasure trove of instruction, wisdom, and the life-giving truths in His Word and He will.

It might not get you a better score on Jeopardy, but the wisdom we find in His truth can keep you out of the real kind of jeopardy—the most disastrous kind. "But if you listen to me, you will be safe and secure without fear of disaster" (Proverbs 1:33 CEV). Safe and without jeopardy. There's your Daily Double.

Pursuing the God of truth, His wisdom, and His direction leads to the place of right answers.

As for the right game show question/answer? Beep-beep-beep, time's up. Maybe instead I should go boil us all some nice, hot brownies.

Added Accents of Colorful Hope from Beth

I know exactly why God put Rhonda and me together for *Fix-Her-Upper*. Because she is the teach, and I am the touch. Not that she doesn't allow her love for others to run deep. She does. She just doesn't let her feelings run all down her face, ruin her mascara, and then leave a mark on the nearest person's sleeve—like I do. I guess you could say I let other people wear my emotions on *their* sleeves.

When it comes to Rhonda and me, I'm like one nail to her nine. She soaks in God's Word, teaches, and encourages…everyone. She points me in the right direction when I'm off track. Actually, we're both directionally challenged. So scratch that metaphor (with the one unpainted nail). But God completes us. We both know people can't fix from the outside what God alone completes on the inside. "Jesus answered, 'I am the way and the truth and the life. No one comes to the Father except through me'" (John 14:13 NLT). As for boiled brownies? Yeah, maybe next time, Rhonda.

Fix Our Eyes on Him

"Let your steadfast love come to me, O Lord, your salvation according to your promise; then shall I have an answer for him who taunts me, for I trust in your word. And take not the word of truth utterly out of my mouth, for my hope is in your rules. I will keep your law continually, forever and ever" (Psalm 119:41-44).

Bringing It Home

In Chapter 3, you were encouraged to write out 2 Timothy 3:16. How about adding verse 17 to make it "artios" and committing it to memory? Remembering what the Word of God does for us moves us all the more to make it part of every day.

Read through Psalm 119. It's 176 verses of Word study stimulus. Underline the "Word" words: *commands, precepts, law, word, testimonies, decrees, statutes*. More?

As you're reading through Psalm 119, note how Word-dependent its writer is. Not because everything in life was perfectly hunky-dory, you'll notice. It's a clue for us, as well, that God's Word is vitally important when things are going well, when things are not going well, and every combination of those two. Choose a verse from Psalm 119 that especially communicates the importance of God's Word. Write it down and put it somewhere you'll see it often.

Chapter Eleven

If the Shiplap Fits

Beth

Keeping up with a fix-her-upper hasn't been easy on my husband Jerry. He knows though, if he builds it, I'll slap paint on it. I'll no doubt accidentally slap some on my sweaty brow, too. Renovations can be chaotic. But then, what's a little chaos as long as there's a big payoff? Right?

Early on I prompted Jerry with my idea. "Doesn't the word 'shiplap' sound cool, Honey? Like an adventure?" That was *before* we sifted through half a lumber yard to find a single straight board. For me, the fun was over with the first splinter.

Still, I couldn't wait to install the fresh look on our dining room walls. Even though we had a couple of minor mishaps, I wanted to be helpful. So, I measured once—Jerry cut twice. I miscalculated again, and my honey pried the metal measuring tape from my "helpful" little fingers. *Hmmm.* With all the extra searching, and cutting, and trim pieces—when the shiplap fit, it was a miracle. When we stepped back to revel in the reveal? *Happy wife, happy life.*

For me, spiritual growth rarely develops when I'm in "the happy." My will doesn't seem to want to break without some struggle. A fresh thought: God is not into breaking a will, but growing a spirit. Growing usually involves some level of discomfort. Just ask a two-year-old.

If the Tiny Shoe Fits

I'd spotted the toddler in front of me at register five in the grocery checkout. The little guy sat in the front of the shopping cart. Since we shared checkout space, I could overhear his mom's reminders. "Now, keep your hands in, and don't put your mouth on the handle." I thought her requests were reasonable. Also, I wondered how many toddlers are reasonable.

I set my to-do list aside and watched the mom pull a lint-covered sucker from her purse. No judging here. *And could they make the checkout lanes any narrower and more toddler friendly?* As fast as his mama started unloading groceries, he began stocking up on…decks of cards? After several decks, his fingers finally made it to a pack of teriyaki jerky. He'd picked his prize. That is, until his mother spotted him.

The little guy was calm as he watched her put the cards away, even though all hopes of his would-be poker party were disappearing. However, as soon as his mother grabbed the jerky, all bets were off. Her argument seemed so big, but his understanding was still toddler-sized. I think she also knew he probably wouldn't like the leathery snack. Moms overflow with this kind of wisdom. Her son's heels kicked the cart. He wanted his jerky-jerky!

The finale was the handle-biting fiasco. I shuddered to think what an exceptionally germy shopping cart handle he was "finale-ing" on. To make things more awkward, the cashier avoided eye contact with both of them—or anyone else. The poor mom looked like she wanted to get out of there. I stared at my to-do list, not really reading it. I did, however, make a mental addition to that list: Take a nap.

I wonder, in the area of tantrums and pouts, am I all that different?

When I Want My Way!

I can identify with that toddler. In addition to our shared love for teriyaki jerky, I'd had a prayer-pout of my own, on the same shopping trip. I had stomped with a heavy heart from the hamburger buns back to the frozen pizza aisle. My silent prayers still churned as I gripped the handle of my shopping cart. Like a toddler clenching jerky, I desperately tried to hang onto what I thought was the best answer.

Not only was I was acting like a two-year-old, but I'd prayed like one, too. I hung my head. I guess if the tiny shoe fits I have to wear it.

We are called to pray, but not simply to get our own way. Paul encourages us to "Pray continually, give thanks in all circumstances; for this is God's will for you in Christ Jesus." (1 Thessalonians 5:17-18 NIV). It's also our attitude in prayer and our motive for praying we need to keep in check. *Lord, don't let me pray myself into a checkout-lane-five kind of spiritual toddler tantrum.*

Spiritual disciplines draw us closer to God. When we consider our motives and attitudes, there is a great heart question we can ask ourselves. Am I praying for His glory and not from my own selfish pride and interests? The prayers of the psalmist are written with deep introspection. "Search me, O God, and know my heart! Try me and know my thoughts! And see if there be any grievous way in me, and lead me in the way everlasting" (Psalm 139:23-24). Our tiny insights are unable to grasp God's big plan in every situation. Contemplating the "everlasting" that is our future, can help us loosen our grip on our right now.

After the birth of our third child, Jerry and I began to feel the busyness of two hectic work schedules, three children and three very lengthy nightly bedtime stories. We agreed—Goldilocks needed to hurry it up a bit. Then one day my husband presented a wild solution while headed out the door to work, "I've been praying about this. Why don't you just quit your job, Honey? It would take a load off us both."

What? Bad idea. My response was bigger than your basic overreaction. My pride had a tantrum and heard a different message from my husband—"My career is more important than yours."

Prayer–The Perfect Fit

Instead of inviting a heart change though, I started searching for an outside solution. With desperate need came a desperate want to have my own way. I tried to change Jerry's mind and heart with prayer. I prayed hard. My need for God in this situation was evident as He began to bring home the truth—I was dependent on my own independence. I was afraid to lean completely on Jerry, and terrified to depend wholly on God.

After months of prayer, something finally clicked. It happened the day I wore two different shoes to work. Actually, one shoe clicked and the other one didn't. And though it had nothing to do with the shoes that was the day I knew Jerry was right. I was refusing the refreshment God was desperately trying to give.

I cried unhappy tears the day I grabbed my briefcase and left twelve happy years of employment. I cried sadder tears the day we found out our daughter had a brain tumor and was given an uncertain prognosis. Good gracious, I cried tears of amazement at the amount of grace and loving intention God lavished on us. He allowed me to have that time with my family and with her. He refreshed my spirit with a gift I didn't even know I wanted. The Lord really does overflow with this kind of wisdom. My unanswered prayers, my sadness, and struggle so often move me toward the blessings of a refreshed soul.

Now, when I step back to revel in the refreshing reveal. Oh, the happy!

Added Accents of Colorful Hope from Rhonda

I remember as a teenager praying so fervently that the Lord would force that one dreamy guy to like me. John was older than I was and so out of my league. He was handsome, sweet, loved Jesus— seriously, this relationship *had* to be what I needed. It probably wasn't even six months later, I was praying just as fervently that the Lord would get me out of that relationship. Yes, with the same handsome, sweet, Jesus-loving guy—who was getting on my last nerve.

What a loving Father. Sometimes He gives us what we desperately need that we never knew we needed. Sometimes He lovingly teaches us by giving us what we desperately want, so He can show us it's not at all what we need. Of one thing we can be sure. Our most desperate need is always Him. And to love Him back with our obedience is always best for us.

Fix Our Eyes On Him

"You have been raised on the Message of the faith and have followed sound teaching. Now pass on this counsel to the followers of Jesus there, and you'll be a good servant of Jesus. Stay clear of silly stories that get dressed up as religion. Exercise daily in God—no spiritual flabbiness, please!" (1 Timothy 4:6-8 The Message).

Bringing It Home

Bible study, discipleship, worship, prayer, sharing Christ, fasting, and attending church are among the many spiritual disciplines. Are there any you've seen the Lord use in big ways in your life? Is there one you've never plugged in you might like to try today?

Is there a prayer you prayed in the past that God didn't answer the way you wanted? Can you see yet how God has used it? Has He ever brought you to a place of spiritual refreshment through an unanswered prayer?

When we give spiritual disciplines a place of importance in our lives, our spirits are refreshed. God built us that way. Can you connect any dots between disciplines you've practiced and new joy, contentment, peace, gratitude—refreshment—you've experienced?

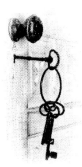

Chapter Twelve

Making the Connections

Rhonda

There's a wood stain, and then there's a shirt stain. I'm afraid I'm not as good at wood.

I was scrubbing furiously, trying to get the hot fudge stain out of my fave workout shirt. And then…the revelation. It was like, "Oh hello, Irony. For a minute I didn't see you there."

Not that the new diet isn't going well or anything. Because I don't think it actually counts as eating badly if you only ate your husband's dessert because you forgot you already ate yours. Doesn't count. Because, "forgot."

It's not that I haven't tapped into all the diet helps presently out there. But I considered I might not be doing it right when I started typing "healthy recipes" into my phone and autocorrect filled in with "pudding cake and cheese dip and lies." Autocorrect can be very judgy.

In the meantime, I've found there are stages a person must go through before accepting a new diet: 1) Denial, 2) Anger, 3) Bargaining, 4) Donut…and then I'm not exactly sure what comes after number four. Very probably another number four.

The other day, after too many fours, I knew I needed human accountability. I may, however, have overdone it there. This afternoon

I was reaching for an oatmeal cream pie when a sniper fired a warning shot.

That's Concerning

Maybe I shouldn't concern myself as much with sniper fire as I do with taking accountability seriously. Would you believe I'm actually scripturally compelled to "be concerned"?

"And let us be concerned about one another in order to promote love and good works, not staying away from our worship meetings, as some habitually do, but encouraging each other, and all the more as you see the day drawing near" (Hebrews 10:24-25 HCSB).

The Greek word translated "be concerned" means to so focus the mind—to consider this thing so carefully—that the result will be the right response. And this "be concerned" is in the present tense, so it's not simply referring to a one-time consideration. We're called to seriously and perpetually think of ways we can promote love and good works, encouraging everyone in our sphere of influence to love Jesus by the way they love and serve each other.

Isn't it almost another irony that we promote those things as we ourselves live in that love? That means our accountability is meant to be loving—no bullets. It's not even to be "judgy." We're to aim more for "stir-uppy"—stirring up others to love and good works, as some versions put it.

This kind of accountability looks best when no one is aiming for condemnation or judgment. Not for wounding or shaming or angering either. Some hurt may inadvertently happen when we lovingly confront. But it should never be our aim. Loving, not sniping. It's good to let humility be the order of the day when someone else is concerned enough to "stir" us as well—even if we don't agree. The truth is, we don't have an auto-correct either.

O Lord, may we love You better as each of us buoys the other. May we inspire and encourage—and be inspired and encouraged—to love You, love each other and to love serving.

Talk about Some Different Connections

Loving each other in this way calls us to be together. Some of us in today's culture aren't quite as good at connecting. Even our conversation has changed.

Instead of the "So how 'bout those Cardinals?" conversation-starters of old, these days it's become something more like, "Hey, what show are you currently binge-watching on Netflix?"

Maybe it's happened to a friend of yours. Maybe it's happened to you. You feel a little like you should get "props" for your good intentions, having sat down to watch just that one pilot episode. But no, no props. Because you've accidentally watched eight seasons. And it's been three days. And you're still wearing the same sweat pants. You try to figure out how much sleep you traded for that show, but your brain is a little foggy. Because…sleep deprivation.

Maybe that's why, you think. That's why somewhere toward the beginning of day two you started thinking of the characters as real people—and why you became convinced you need grief counseling after that one especially shocking and devastating plot twist.

Ironic, isn't it, that at a time in our culture when it's perfectly acceptable to watch hour upon hour of a television show, we still freak out if a Sunday morning church service goes seven minutes over? The Sunday response is like the agitation of a binge-watcher with a waffling Internet connection.

What about a Real Connection?

Jesus-followers need an influencing touch from each other that's more real—more intense, more enduring—than any glut-watch. It should go without saying, right? Yet it doesn't always show up in the typical practice of the average follower. It should also go without saying that I want to follow Christ more intently than I ever follow anything fake. But I'm going on record anyway.

Paul told his student Timothy to "command and teach" in 1 Timothy 4:11 and then specified to "devote yourself to public reading of Scripture, to exhortation, to teaching," in verse 13. Public. Every believer needs connection—real people who can nurture, hold accountable, teach, correct, fellowship, encourage—all those things that happen in the local church.

There's also an instruction in Hebrews 13 to "Remember our leaders, those who spoke to you the word of God. Consider the outcome of their way of life, and imitate their faith" (vs. 7). We can't remember our church leaders, listen to the teaching or imitate their faith if we don't personally watch. Dare I say, *binge*-watch?

A give-and-receive fellowship/learning involvement, as well as soul-protection, unfolds in the church. Our Lord designed it that way. It pleases Him. Just a few verses later in Hebrews 13 we read, "Do not neglect to do good and to share what you have, for such sacrifices are pleasing to God. Obey your leaders and submit to them, for they are keeping watch over your souls" (vv. 16-17).

We're wise when we give the church the place of significance in our lives it merits. It's the "not staying away" part of that Hebrews 10:25 (HCSB) command: "not staying away from our worship meetings." Active involvement in doing life with a local church body is vital to a victorious faith-life. And it's not merely "watching." It's about doing.

Our shows will eventually end. The church? Never. There's no substitute for obediently connecting with real people. It's how we're called to live.

A renovated home is designed to be lived in. Faith is designed to be lived in and out.

Getting lost in a three-day TV binge, not so much. Might as well not even try to stay on that diet. Never mind the four stages of donuts or whatever. Because I've heard you can get to the third day and suddenly find out you've eaten nothing but Lucky Charms the whole time. And that you ran out of milk on day two.

Added Accents of Colorful Hope from Beth

Remember how in many of the chapters we've hammered on the fact that spiritual refreshment and renovation occurs from the inside-out? Well, Rhonda's right. An accountability friend is a great way to add those final touches to our spiritual insides. A friend with an eye for divine, shares our concerns and efforts without pointing a painted finger at our flaws. It's great to have someone lean in with some "let's do this" prayer-power and encouragement.

Because I've seen people walk away from God. It isn't pretty. It's a heart in a state of ill repair—and by the way—we can all get there! That's why I've had an accountability friend for many years and count her a totally needed and gracious blessing. Patsy is a friend who helps me maintain a vital prayer life, spruce my spiritual fervor, and freshen my faith in and out. Although she may need a ton of prayer. I didn't title this book fix-her-upper by accident.

Fix Our Eyes on Him

"Let the word of Christ dwell in you richly, teaching and admonishing one another in all wisdom, singing psalms and hymns and spiritual songs, with thankfulness in your hearts to God" (Colossians 3:16).

Bringing It Home

Got a Bible-preaching, Jesus-loving church home? Are you regular in attendance? If yes, pray for opportunities to encourage others to come with you. If no, why not make a commitment today to go three months (yes, three months) without missing a Sunday. New research indicates that it takes 66 days to form a habit. Here's a habit that's worth the effort.

Pray about new ways the Lord might want you to be involved in your church and in other ministries He might be calling you to.

If you don't have a prayer list that helps you keep track of the needs of others, start one today. Who can you pray for? Who is the Lord calling you to exercise a "focused concern" about, as Hebrews 10:24-25 indicates we should have? If you already have a list, read over and pray through it right now. Ask the Lord again where He might like you to focus your concern in prayer for others.

Part *Four*

Refurbish!

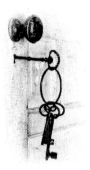

Chapter Thirteen

The Perfect Finish

Rhonda

You can tell a lot about people by the way they finish a project. Or don't. I think I've probably already given you enough hints for you to figure out that I'm a "don't-er."

Interestingly, you can also tell a lot about people by the way they do their laundry. I have friends, for instance, who have certain days they designate as "laundry days." I confess, I'm probably much more impressed by that than any grown woman should be. My laundry days? They usually happen on whatever days I realize I have to make a choice: Wash a load, or become one of those people who goes to Wal-Mart in pajama pants.

I'm further impressed by my friends who go the extra mile, laundry-wise. They—are you ready for this?—*pre-treat*. They do it like it's a normal thing people do. But do you know what pre-treating is? It's doing laundry before you actually do the laundry. There's something remarkably intentional and impressively diligent about that.

I have other friends who go beyond that and carry one of those pen-things with them so they can pre-treat before a stain makes it to the laundry room. They're essentially doing laundry before they're even home. It borders on laundry lunacy.

It All Comes Out in the Wash

It probably won't shock you to know that when I'm having dinner at a restaurant and hot fudge drips down my sweater, I'm not thinking about laundry. You know what I'm thinking? Fudge. And if I scrape the fudge off my sweater, it's not a pre-treatment. It's a fudge salvage.

Some people do laundry with great forethought. I do laundry with great afterthought.

Of course, there's regular forethought. And then there's the forethought of God. His is a whole different basket of laundry. We're told in Titus 3:4-5 that "when the goodness and loving kindness of God our Savior appeared, he saved us." How vital it is to stay intentional and deliberate about remembering He planned our salvation. That passage continues, "not because of works done by us in righteousness, but according to his own mercy, by the washing of regeneration and renewal of the Holy Spirit, whom he poured out on us richly through Jesus Christ our Savior" (vv. 5-6).

No kind of laundering would ever make us clean enough apart from that "washing of regeneration," the saving work of Jesus Christ. We can't do enough deeds, attend enough services—we can't pray enough, or pay enough—to earn what is freely given by His mercy.

I know what you're probably thinking. This is an oversimplified, everybody-already-knows-it, fact of the faith. Yet how many times do we overcomplicate the Gospel? It's just Jesus. His amazing, pre-thought grace. "For by grace you have been saved through faith. And this is not your own doing; it is the gift of God" (Ephesians 2:8).

Even those of us who've been around the Christian block a few times need to be reminded to trust His grace. It's easy to get off-track, concentrating on all the "good" we might be doing, forgetting the One we're doing it for. Embracing our own lack of ability to do anything of lasting value is at the same time embracing His ability to do more than we could ever imagine. And that's something we need to embrace anew every day. Oh, His marvelous, everyday provision!

The best renovation experts don't slap another layer of paint on woodwork thick with old, chipped, worn-out layers from years gone by. They strip the woodwork down to the original wood, no matter how much effort it takes, restoring the sheen and glow the carpenter intended.

The connection is clear, isn't it?

To the Finish

I like to hang onto that thought on days I feel like I'm leaving too many things undone. Ever had one of those days? I had several in a row. And by "several," I mean at least ten years' worth. They were days of never feeling quite...*finished*. I would get to the end of the day and think, *what did I actually get done?* It wasn't that I hadn't accomplished anything. But when you have five children in seven years, there will no doubt be days when, while you're trying to salvage the toaster (the one someone used to try to toast Milk Duds), one of the other kids tells you your toddler covered the cat with pudding and your first-grader just threw up in the toy box.

Without resorting to laundry stories, I could tell an extra-large load of tales of finishing a day without really finishing what I felt I should've finished. And if I did mention laundry, I would have to wonder how many mornings I felt relatively okay about the fact that the kids were digging through the *clean* basket of laundry for something to wear instead of the *dirty* one. Every day seemed to be a new experience in unfinished business.

Now the kids are grown and I'm in a new season. At the end of a day, there's just about as much I feel I've left hanging (and no, that's not a laundry reference). Deadlines, tapings, contacts and contracts—and, oh my goodness, there's *still* laundry.

I've made a discovery through all the years of unfinished business. I've discovered that I fret the most about what I'm not accomplishing when I'm struggling to accomplish it all in my own strength. And that's when I focus on all the wrong accomplishments anyway.

The Author and "Finisher"

There's a recalibration of the focus and a completely different outlook on those worries over what I haven't yet done. It happens when I realize that everything truly vital in this life—everything worth finishing—has already been accomplished by the "Author and *Finisher*" of our faith. At each point, when I surrender and let the Finisher do the finishing, let the Completer do the completing, I can stop the sweating and experience His peace.

"Now may the God of peace who brought up our Lord Jesus from the dead, that great Shepherd of the sheep, through the blood of the everlasting covenant, make you complete in every good work to do His will, working in you what is well pleasing in His sight, though Jesus Christ, to whom be glory forever and ever. Amen" (Hebrews 13:20-21 NKJV).

He is the Completer of every good work—and He does that finishing work "in" us. He is faithful to finish the works that really count—as faithful as He is to accomplish the saving work in us. When the Father completed His redemptive plan through the sacrificial death of His Son on the cross, the most glorious words of all time reverberated across eternity: *"It is finished."*

Imagine a home renovation that never gets finished. What chaos! That can't happen when the project is, well, us.

Resting in His finished work gives us an entirely different take on the unfinished projects, the looming deadlines, the stains—even the toasted Milk Duds. It moves the "finish line" to a reachable spot, one He will reach for us and in us in the most glorious way. I think we can call that our big finish.

Added Accents of Colorful Hope from Beth

Father, You are the true finisher of our faith. You are faithful to see our hearts through. Despite circumstance, we can have the peace and contentment that comes from knowing You are enough. We don't have to search. We don't need to wander. We can rest. Rest in the truth that You are perfect and will not leave anything undone. Not our hearts. And especially not our souls. Help us to be thirsty and hungry for the right things, looking for satisfaction and contentment in You alone. We can only be made whole by You. Whatever our felt need, we ask that You meet us…and then complete us. In Your precious name, amen.

Fix Our Eyes on Him

"Always in every prayer of mine for you all making my prayer with joy, because of your partnership in the gospel from the first day until now. And I am sure of this, that he who began a good work in you will bring it to completion at the day of Jesus Christ" (Philippians 1:4-6).

Bringing It Home

The Gospel. So complex in its simplicity. "It's just Jesus." Stop and pray right now for the glorious gift of grace that is our salvation.

Take a look at your to-do list. Are there things it that are undone and that are frustrating away your joy? Are the things that are frustrating you things that you want to get done, or things the Lord has called you to do? Sometimes we put things on the list that He hasn't called us to. If that's the case for you, pray about what you might cross off that list. Other times, we can get frustrated because we feel it's taking us to long to accomplish a task—even though we feel sure He's called us to do it. Just because it's a calling doesn't mean it's always going to be easy. Recognizing that it's something He wants you to do, however, changes the way you approach it. You can know for sure that if He calls you to it, He will empower it.

Pray through that to-do list right now, from top to bottom, whether it's a written list or a mental one. Ask the Lord what should stay and what should go. Lean on Him to empower you "to the finish."

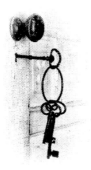

Chapter Fourteen

Miracle Makeover

Beth

No matter how hard we try, home makeovers last f-o-r-e-v-e-r at the Duewel house.

My husband and I think the project is finally complete, but then we realize one little detail remains undone. That's what happened last year. The "little" detail turned out to be several oak boards still missing from our floor re-do. That naked section of floor—sad, bare particle board that it was—looked practically perfect, though, once we covered it with an adorable gray and white chevron rug. It's funny, it looked so complete we totally forgot what we hid under there. I guess the chevron is in the details.

There is another makeover mystery at our house. If there's an unfinished project that's out of sight, it's also out of mind. A kind of detail-dementia, I think. For instance, we may have a door that opens and shuts, but it can still be missing one significant component—like a doorknob. Detail-dementia. We do have good friends who come over to offer courteous reminders like, "No door knob yet, huh?"

So, it's been a few…um…*years.* Still no doorknob. Maybe my memory for details has slipped through the cracks of those undone floorboards. Honestly, I've learned to count it a true miracle if all the details of our makeovers get completed before we need the next one.

I'm so grateful we serve a God who masters details with perfection. Never a transformation incomplete. In fact, Scripture reminds us that we are each one of His complete details, so to speak, and that we are always on His mind. "See I have written your name on the palms of my hands," (Isaiah 49:16 NLT). This gives a whole new meaning to the word "handmade." Intimate thoughts of us are always before God. Wow.

Handmade

That's why I cringe when I think of the many times I've criticized my own reflection, only seeing faults and flaws.

I was pretty young the first time I thought I needed a major makeover. It was picture day—sixth grade. And my hair was just too plain. All the girls flocked to the bathroom before getting in line for pictures, each one pulling out her fine-toothed black comb. They all primped and perfected while I had one impulsive thought, "I must curl my bangs."

I wetted my bangs until they grew limp down my forehead. And then I wrapped. And wrapped. I wound the comb tight enough to raise my eyebrows—I looked so surprised. I realized much too late there was no undoing my mistake. Surprise! The comb had swallowed my hair whole.

Now I look back and laugh. Then though, insecurities and doubt about who I was printed itself in the year book and in my mind.

It's as if I heard God question, "I created *her*?" It's a question that can still tangle itself up in my self-worth. My insecurities try to break down what God desires to build up. Me. His design. I want to change much about who I am. Quirky. Impatient. Quick to anger, quick to doubt God and quick to become mercilessly critical of the person I am—even though I am a woman made in God's image. And just a side note: I don't care how innocent kid scissors may seem, they should never be your go-to makeover tool. They are not kid friendly. They are not adult friendly either. You can take my word on this one.

I also know the more significant point isn't why God made us, but the way He made us. We can find security when we meditate on the way He created us with such intense affection and with perfect purpose. God created us. Even an eyelash is purposed and planned.

"So God created man in his own image, in the image of God he created him; male and female he created them" (Genesis 1:27). This verse is alive with identity. God created. He shaped. He fashioned. In this next verse from Psalm 139, God's Word confirms this about His creation: We are not unplanned or unknown to Him.

"My frame was not hidden from you, when I was being made in secret, intricately woven in the depths of the earth. Your eyes saw my unformed substance, in your book were written, every one of them, the days that were formed for me, when as yet there was none of them" (Psalm 139:13-16).

Clearly, this sneak peek into our creation supports God's big reveal. We have no business questioning why we were made. Because we were handmade. We were created with intention *and* attention to every single cell.

As in the story of Elle.

When I was Being Made in Secret

Elle is the five-year-old daughter of friends, Lance and Robin George. When you see her, you notice her adorable, mischievous smile. It's as if she already knows the winding path to her existence. But she's too young to know her creation is an example of God's detailed design. She doesn't realize she's a miraculous reminder of His Sovereign hand in mastering creation. She's just busy being Elle Grace George.

After seven years of trying everything to have a child, Lance and Robin prayerfully considered in vitro fertilization. Due to the doctors' concern for multiple births, and a question concerning the overall health of the fourth embryo, they suggested only three of the four harvested embryos be implanted. The fourth embryo was frozen. Since embryos donated aren't typically stored and frozen for a period longer than three years, Lance included a note stating, "Please contact us before destroying." Then they prayed.

Intrinsically Woven in the Depths of the Earth

The Georges were heartbroken when they discovered the IVF procedure had failed. After the tears, though, came their steadfast resolve to cling to faith and hold on for whatever the Lord might have for them. I'm so thankful for some of the things Robin told me from the depths of this grief. "God will not leave us undone with pain." So true. Neither will He slap us with a thoughtless gloss or fresh coat of temporary. I'm reminded of the words David uses in verse 13 of Psalm 139, "intricately woven." Or in other words, complicatedly interlaced. These words affirm God's intention and the creative attention to detail He gives to our making.

Lining up my thinking with words like "intricately woven" helps me hear God's proclamation, "I created her!" And it doesn't stop there. If the Creator of my DNA has a purpose for making me so complicated—crazy bangs and all—He must have a purpose in the ways He chooses to form and grow me spiritually. I can be sure, I'm His miracle, too.

Growing isn't always easy—even for a miracle. But we can find security when we think about who made us. We can experience a refurbished life. Because there is also repair—healing—in the simple act of trusting God to do the whole makeover. All. By. Himself. Start to finish. As He did in the lives of Lance and Robin.

The Georges became pregnant shortly after the failed IVF attempt. No medications. No procedures. On August 16th of 2002, they gave birth to their son, Case, and then were blessed to have another boy, Colton, in January of 2005.

In Your Book Were Written

God pays perfect attention to His creation. It was time for His big reveal. He remembered Elle.

He'd already declared the days for her. In fact, the Georges thought their embryo—the fourth frozen embryo—had been adopted out after three years to another infertile couple in need. But she hadn't.

Nor had she been discarded. Elle's embryo sat frozen on a shelf for nine years! Way beyond the point of being considered viable by the experts. One day, Robin received a phone call, "Mrs. George, we wanted to let you know we were cleaning out some old files and discovered a note instructing us to please notify you before destroying your embryo."

Elle was born nine years past her due date, but in God's perfect time on October 22, 2011.

It's almost like a beautiful fairytale. Except that it's real. He is a God of miracle makeovers in so many ways. But unlike some makeovers I know, with undone details and missing elements, we can place our confidence in God's miracle makeovers lasting f-o-r-e-v-e-r. And if you ever question that God made the unique you, just remember this story of Elle Grace George. Her parents realized several days *after* naming her that her initials live true to God's eye for detail…and a little humor: E-G-G.

Added Accents of Colorful Hope from Rhonda

What a beautiful reminder and delightful celebration of a God who is so big, so great, and so powerful. He is the only one who can create something out of nothing. He's the only one who can create some*one*. And He is the same "only one" who can accomplish the miracle of refurbishing a soul. *O Lord, thank You for this reminder that You have all power to create and to save, and that Your plan is intricate, loving—amazing!*

Fix Our Eyes on Him

"You know me inside and out, you know every bone in my body; You know exactly how I was made, bit by bit, how I was sculpted from nothing into something. Like an open book, you watched me grow from conception to birth; all the stages of my life were spread out before you, the days of my life all prepared before I'd even lived one day" (Psalm 139:15-16 MSG).

Bringing It Home

Have you ever questioned how or why you were created? Read Psalm 139:14 again. Commit it to memory.

Read verses 15-16 in that chapter as well. Is there any corner of insecurity in your life where you find yourself asking if God really made you that way? Meet those places of insecurity with these verses that tell you the truth of how you were created with forethought and purpose.

Are you willing to allow God to work His miracles in your life? Write down five verses that speak to His power to work miracles and to our well-placed trust in Him.

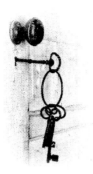

Chapter Fifteen

Balanced Design—Oh So Divine!

Rhonda

I hear lots of people talk about achieving just the right "balance" in their home design. Of course, when is balance not a good thing?

Have you ever had one of those world-tipping inner ear malfunctions? It's about the worst kind of imbalance. It started small when it happened to me. My body kept trying to lean to one side. I expected someone to come up behind me and stick a couple of sugar packets under my left foot to keep me from wobbling.

Then, as inner-ear malfunctions are wont to do, the imbalance accelerated. Suddenly the world was very— How can I describe it? Very *"Star Ship Enterprise."* The kind of *Enterprise* where a space anomaly has the ship flailing back and forth. I felt fine when I was lying down. But it was a busy season. I'd been meeting myself coming and going and lying down made me remember everything I needed to do.

Verti-coming and Verti-going

At one point, I thought I could sneak up on a couple of to-do list items without my ears knowing. I was moving slowly, oh so slowly…when suddenly, "Red Alert!" Thrusters were off-line. It felt like I was boldly verti-going where no one has verti-gone before.

Fortunately, I'm not a great housekeeper when I'm overly busy so there was a nice, soft pile of laundry in the floor. I crash-landed there. I had several minutes of contemplative time, staring at the ceiling, waiting for it to stop spinning and for the nausea to let up. In those moments, I decided that resting—even with a big to-do list—wasn't such a bad thing.

Regularly, I have to force myself to reevaluate my busyness. To step back from it and analyze it. Sometimes I do it by choice. Sometimes, I confess, the Lord compels me. At least once, while lying in a pile of laundry.

Balance often requires more than just reorganizing a schedule. We've mentioned that it requires making decisions about what God has called me to do and what He hasn't. The truth is, the Lord will never call me to do anything He won't give me enough time to do. The schedule becomes overwhelming when He gives me a to-do list, and then I add more to it. I end up with no balance, overdoing things that don't matter and underdoing those that do. There aren't enough sugar packets to fix that kind of imbalance.

Careful in How We Walk

When we're persistently out of balance, we find ourselves vulnerable to burn-out, illness, depression—*shields up, red alert!* And let's be clear. Stepping back and reevaluating doesn't mean we put ourselves first. Actually, when we seek *the Lord* first, we find ourselves free to serve Him better, and to serve Him more carefully and intentionally. That's exactly how we're called to serve. Paul tells us in Ephesians 5:15-17, "Pay careful attention, then, to how you walk—not as unwise people but as wise—making the most of the time, because the days are evil. So don't be foolish, but understand what the Lord's will is" (HCSB).

Sometimes wise-walking looks more like lying down. It's listening and seeking—even resting. Paying "careful attention" will keep us from stumbling out of the will of God.

So rather than having every moment filled with busyness, life is better when I seek Him first, and then just plain give Him space to work. Yes, "space." All of it. Because that kind of space is the *final, final* frontier.

If there is a final, final, *final* frontier, it's heaven. What a great balance-giver it is when we spend less time fretting over the sometimes-out-of-whack, temporary messiness here, and more time thinking about how Jesus wants to use our "right now," and contemplating, as well, our glorious future with Him in heaven.

I've Got a Mansion, Just Over the Grill-Top

Messiness is obviously an area where I have some expertise. I don't believe it's true, but someone once told me that a house perpetually and perfectly well-kept is a sign of an "uninteresting" life. Again, not true. But for people who believe it, I might be one of the most *fascinating* people they'll ever meet.

Sometimes, to get inspired to get my house in order, I look up cleaning and organizing tips on Pinterest. Next thing I know, I'm thinking about DIY-ing something amazing. It has nothing whatsoever to do with cleaning my house, but still. It's not like I can't use one more idea for building a grill gazebo—that will never, ever happen.

At some point, I do realize I have to get real and tidy up. I was gathering shoes from the family room not too long ago and chuckle-whined to my daughter, "Your dad has three pairs of shoes in here." Then, "Mercy! Two pairs of your brother's shoes over there. *Ten* man-shoes in one room!"

My daughter, Kaley, who is always at ease with the clever comebacks, answered, "In my father's house are many man-shoes."

Even at its tidiest, my house? Never uninteresting.

Not Exactly Balanced and Tidy

It's even more interesting that, spiritually-speaking, we live in an ever-messy, off-balance world. Not just a bit of disorder now and then. Not simply a little dusty here or there. Fallen. A place where immorality and depravity are a lot closer to the norm than right living and love for God. In all its messiness, our world doesn't merely avoid loving God. There are those who are passionate in their attempts to remove His influence. It's not exactly "mansion, sweet mansion" here.

Jesus said, "In my Father's house are many mansions: if it were not so, I would have told you. I go to prepare a place for you. And if

I go and prepare a place for you, I will come again, and receive you unto myself; that where I am, there ye may be also" (John 14:2-3 KJV). It's a passage that thrills our souls. Not the man-shoes—or even the mansions. It thrills because while we're dealing with the mess of this world, we're reminded of the treasure of living in the presence of God.

I do love the thought of a place "prepared." A clutterless place far removed from everything messy. Better yet, there's a reception. "I will receive you to myself." What will make heaven the sweetest home? We'll be "received"—by Jesus.

In an untidy world, dirty little distractions can threaten to sidetrack those of us who seek to faithfully follow Christ toward that reception. It's vital that we not allow any of the world's mess to block out the glorious eternal.

His Presence—All the Balance We Need

A few verses later, Jesus says, "I will ask the Father, and He will give you another Counselor to be with you forever. He is the Spirit of truth. The world is unable to receive Him because it doesn't see Him or know Him. But you do know Him, because He remains with you and will be in you" (John 14:16-17 HCSB).

That's real life-balance. It's how we focus and follow: His remaining presence! The same Lord who promises to receive us indwells us by His Holy Spirit. Oh, what a gift His presence is. It changes everything! For the hope of our glorious future. For life, here and now.

For the well-balanced and altogether organized—and for those of us who are, let's say, a little too *fascinating*.

Added Accents of Colorful Hope from Beth

Rhonda, texting me after I'd sent her my mailing address: *Is that 777000? Seems like a long hwy #.*

Me: *Sorry. Accidentally added some #'s. I'm an awful multi-tasker. Also I need to keep my glasses on. I lost them. In the bathroom. So I couldn't see when I texted you (I was still in the bathroom). Bathroom texting: bad. And I need one of those long necklace-things to tether my glasses to myself.*

Rhonda: *I'm picturing the mailman taking that package zillions of miles out of his way, still searching for hwy 777000. No more bathroom texting for you. Lol.*

Over-busy. It's rarely a good thing. Rarely a God thing either. When we're too busy for the important, little things, are we sure we're taking time for the big, God things? Are we making time for His big heart changes? Or are we too busy to notice His attempts to refurbish and renovate our lives? Today: Engage with God. Maybe even leave your phone *and* your to-do list…in the bathroom.

Fix Our Eyes on Him

> "'Now therefore, if I have found favor in your sight, please show me now your ways, that I may know you in order to find favor in your sight. Consider too that this nation is your people.' And he said, 'My presence will go with you, and I will give you rest'" (Exodus 33:13-14).

Bringing It Home

Have you ever felt out of balance, busyness-wise? Feeling it now? Have you or do you see it leading to burnout, illness or depression? Seek the Lord right now. Ask Him to give you the balance you need. Don't hesitate to seek counsel or medical help where you need to as well. That is not weakness. It's very often wisdom.

If now is one of those out-of-whack times, make a list of some concrete things you can do to ease some of your stress.

Contemplating our glorious future with Him can be perspective-giving when we're overwhelmed. That beautiful place where we will be "received" by Jesus. Thank Him right now for what He has in store for you—things we can hardly imagine. Ask Him to give you a balanced view of the temporary here and now, and your heavenly future.

Don't miss the balance, perspective, wisdom and peace our Comforter gives. The Holy Spirit of God dwells in you. Thank Him right now for His presence.

Chapter Sixteen

The Big Fix

Beth

I admit, being a mom of three has encouraged the belief that I'm a fixer. Moms hear, "Fix it, Mom!" and tend to interpret it as, "My mom is a superhero." That's what I heard, anyway. It felt all the more urgent when the cry was coming from my frantic then-five-year-old's quivering lips. My daughter begged me to save the day—or more precisely, save the butterfly. Brooklyn had found the monarch in our yard, its wing torn completely in two. Did you know Scotch Tape really isn't the big fix for a broken butterfly wing? Ah well, you can't blame me for trying. It's tough to watch your child hurting, flapping and flailing in the grass. I had to at least *try* to fix it.

Every mom wants to sport a giant "S" on her shirt. We want to be super-something. We start to nudge ourselves from deep inside, thinking, "If I can keep my eye on the target, aim for the best-mom-ever mark, surely I'll get it right." Day-in and day-out, we make play-dough from scratch, and brownies from…well, from a box, but still. We volunteer at track meets and help with school projects. We give all of our energy, and sacrifice all our quiet potty-breaks to our kids. Always on the go. Sometimes we're grabbing the tape. Sometimes we grab a kid's forgotten sack lunch. And we go.

When I saw another chance to try on a supersized "S," I was going to take it. My oldest daughter, Brittany, called home. "Mom, I forgot my lunch. Can you please bring it to school?" I was not going to miss another shot at super-ness.

The Forgotten Fix

Hmmm, getting it to her in time meant no time for a shower. I glanced in the mirror and realized I needed to at least do my hair before I headed to the school. Or my hair just needed to do something. Besides stand on end. My original plan was to have a morning-ful of laundry. I didn't need to look great for that. But getting that lunch to school in the hurriest way meant no time for getting cleaned up and cute. I was going in as-is, even the hair.

In the wild rush, I was halfway to the school before I realized I'd forgotten one thing. The one thing that was the very purpose of the trip. Brittany's lunch was back at home, sitting right where I'd left it on the counter. I'd put it by my keys where I was sure to see it while whizzing out the door. Nope. Oh well, I figured I could swing through a fast-food restaurant instead and treat Brittany to her favorite fruit parfait. I pulled in and ordered. I even got extra apple pies for her friends. Extra napkins, too, for any unforeseen messes. Because a super-mom does that sort of thing.

I'd hoped to just drop off the "lunch" and pies and run home to messy bliss. But, no, it seemed I'd broken a school rule. The lady in the office was quick to point it out, peering her squinty, judgy eyes at me over her glasses. No fast-food bags allowed. Only very plain, very brown paper bags. Just like the one I left sitting on the counter. Ugh.

As I walked out of the office, my daughter giggled at the slipup and thanked me for trying. I shared a snort-laugh with her. "What are moms for, anyway?" *if not to tempt you with fast food you can't have.*

Super Fix-It-Ness

On the way home, though, I couldn't ignore a feeling of failure, despite all the things I'd attempted. Maybe it was the way the office worker examined me, eyeing my hurry-hair. Or the frustration over my own forgetfulness. Either way, trying to fix everything was getting to be too much. I know that feeling of "too much" can wash over a mom from time to time, but this time it felt like it wouldn't wash off. There had been too much forgetfulness. Too many things missed. Too much financial stress. And for sure, too much homework!

The night before, I'd had to face a frustrating fact. I was flunking my kids' high school math. My husband, the math go-to guy, wasn't available, and I knew the kids had to be near desperate to ask help from me. Asking me for help while I was fixing dinner was even riskier. Math and meatloaf really don't mix.

If I could go back to high school, I would heed my teacher's shaking finger and stern warning: "Someday you'll need to know this!" I had no clue "someday" would be when my own children asked me about algebra. "Oh, sorry, Honey. Mommy doesn't know. I was daydreaming during that class." But supermoms aren't supposed to need help. They just try harder, right?

Wrestling with those feelings of failure, I recognized a flaw in myself. In my super-fix-it-ness tendencies, I was attempting to be every single big fix in my children's lives, when only the Savior can. I've tried to wear perfection—I've tried on Holy. I've eyed the shiny, "Super S" status.

In that moment, I recognized, in great relief, that I wasn't alone in my struggle, not even alone in my chaos. God was very present. He never once stopped caring for my children. The problem was that there were moments I stopped trusting Him with them, and stopped inviting Him in to help. The book of Isaiah reminds, "This is what the Sovereign LORD, the Holy One of Israel, says: 'In repentance and rest is your salvation, in quietness and trust is your strength, but you would have none of it'" (Isaiah 30:15 NIV).

The Forever Fix

With all my running and doing and taping and fixing, I had to ask myself a hard question. Did I spend enough time kneeling? All attempts at being God in my children's lives backfired and left me with remorse, fatigue, and a broken-down, hassled spirit. In Rhonda's Chapter 10, my note emphasized the completion of our soul by God alone. Rhonda and I both know it's impossible to fix from the outside what God alone completes from the inside. That is much of the passion behind these pages.

Refurbishment comes when we take off the "S," put it down, and step away. Whatever we do, we are to do it as an offering of love to the only One who is Holy. "Whether ye eat or drink or whatsoever ye do, do all to the glory of God" (1 Corinthians 10:31 KJV).

C. S. Lewis reminds us of this kind of restoration in *The Weight of Glory* (Macmillan, 1949). "All our merely natural activities will be accepted, if they are offered to God, even the humblest, and all of them, even the noblest, will be sinful if they are not." It's true. My offering is acceptable to Him when all of what I do is for His glory.

Offering love to my children, though that love is often imperfect, is still offering glory to God. Giving God the whole of my day, even in my imperfection, and recognizing Him in the small, shines a light on His big splendor. It fixes my eyes on the right mark. Not simply the best-mom-ever mark, but fixes my eyes on Him. It takes away the need to try to impress with the "S"—and all its added stress.

Letting God wear Holy will refurbish our thinking and our lives. We don't have to be the fixer in the lives of our children. We don't have to do a thing but rest. Whew!

Praising the God who is the Big Fix! Supernatural. Sovereign. Savior. Sustainer. And He is eternally sufficient. He changes and repairs us for eternal purposes. I'm so glad, too, because I can barely keep up with the laundry on any given day, not to mention the homework. Now it's off to the store to get more brown bags. Plain ones, of course.

Added Accents of Colorful Hope from Rhonda

"Look! Up in the sky! It's a bird! It's a plane!" OK, let's get real. Any "S" you see on my chest is probably a ketchup stain. I don't need a lot of convincing that I'm not perfect. But I love the reminder here that I don't have to be. Not as a wife. Not as a mom. Not as a follower of Jesus. That's what grace is all about. The fourth verse of "Amazing Grace" by John Newton (1779) reminds me:

"The Lord has promised good to me,
His Word my hope secures;
He will my shield and portion be
As long as life endures."

Our "Shield." Love the "S." It's super.

Fix Our Eyes on Him

"Oh, the depth of the riches and wisdom and knowledge of God! How unsearchable are his judgments and how inscrutable his ways! For who knows the mind of the Lord, or who has been his counselor? Or who has given a gift to him that he might be repaid? For from him and through him and to him are all things. To him be the glory forever. Amen" (Romans 11:33-36).

Bringing It Home

Theologians agree, our bottom-line purpose in life is to glorify God. Today, offer up all you do—whether you're eating or sleeping, or spending time with your family—for the glory of God, intentionally giving praise in your offering to His splendor.

Praying for and with our children is one of the purest forms of love we can offer. Here are some Scriptures you can pray over your children. Insert their names as you pray. Ephesians 3:14-19, Romans 10:9, 13. Psalm 119:9-16.

Look up Hebrews 13:15-16. What does each verse speak of sacrificing to God? What do we need to offer up? What do these verses say about how God views our sacrifice?

Part *Five*

Revive!

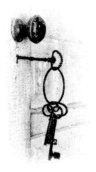

Chapter Seventeen

A Peace of Work

Beth

Simple touches make a house a home and a place I both love and like. So when I saw a simple barn door constructed of chippy-white-wood and beautiful oak, I knew it was the "look" I wanted. Then I begged Jerry to construct a door just like it to slide across the entrance of my office. Okay lovelies, I figured something out. Beauty *is* in the eye of the barn-door-beholder.

What does the door look like? Conjure a picture in your mind of messy and nice. And then a mix of perfectly imperfect. A-door-able. A beautiful piece of work! Although your idea of beauty may not match mine, or visa-versa, because everyone is different and so is their viewpoint.

My particular perspective? Well…oh, gosh, how do I describe it? Eclectic? I meticulously gather my eye for design from a broad and diverse range of sources, a.k.a., home renovation re-runs and thrift shops. No wonder the first time my father-in-law saw the barn-siding turned office door, he couldn't wrap his mind around the "look" I wanted. Or contain his curiosity.

"Did you mean to make it like this?" He rubbed his hand across the rough wood. "I thought maybe you weren't finished."

It seems my husband and I constructed something on purpose that looks like a complete accident. For me though, my new office door was a perfect mistake. It's all in how you look at it.

Because life isn't pressed out and perfect. Life's full of potential. A beautiful piece of work in progress. When we seek to see deeper than the surface of circumstance we can find more beauty, more love, more hope, and definitely more peace. But only if we are seeking more God.

Bigger is Better

Because bigger than how we view a barn door, is how we view the largeness of a perfect God. For instance when I was younger my perspective of God was huge. So was the memory of the backyard I played in as a kid. The soft grass was two kickball teams wide. The buckeye tree we climbed touched the tip of heaven. Recently though, I stopped to visit my childhood home. And compared to how I remembered it, it looked like the sprawling yard was now a small square of grass, and the tree barely tipped twenty feet. Let alone heaven. I've simply grown up and everything else has shrunk.

Our view of God can shrink too. How large we see Him affects how much we trust Him and His provision. After all, a little God can't handle our huge problems. He can't take care of us, or love us in a large way, or begin to provide the great peace we need to make it through the toughest days.

Peace of Mind

Now, let's take a moment to revive this big thought, "You keep him in perfect peace whose mind is stayed on you, because he trusts you." (Isaiah 26:3-4). When we fix our minds on God, He nurtures us in absolute peace. In effect, God knows the "look" He desires and offers peace when we look to Him to provide it. Pleasing peace.

Thank goodness God doesn't expect perfection in exchange for His peace-filled provision. Too bad we allow our need for perfection to make us think otherwise.

Perfection can act like a blindfold we put on and then tie in a knot. Believe me. I tied my perfection-driven blindfold in a nice, tidy, super-tight, knot and then bumped into everything thinking, *"I can't stand the messy in life. The flaws. Or the dings in my day!"* I stubbed my toe enough to know that the wont for perfect robs our joy and blinds our peace-perspective.

Seeing is Believing

Peace of mind comes from knowing that perfection does not play a role in our calm. But trust does. Again, Isaiah reminds us that we can't trust everything we see in our peripheral vision. Mostly because it may not tell us the truth about the beauty ahead. Especially when we are seeing life through the slant of sleepy eyes, rough days, and uncertain circumstances. The truth about God's peace is found in His Word, "Peace I leave with you; my peace I give to you." (John 14:27). According to Isaiah we see God is a peace keeper. Now, we are reminded He is a peace giver.

So the beliefs we hold should reflect facts about God. Like: God is always at work. He is always trustworthy, always willing to love, and forever willing to listen. He is a, "…Wonderful Counselor, Mighty God, Everlasting Father, Prince of Peace." (Isaiah 9:6). He is peace for you. He is peace for me. With all this peace then, why do we lose sleep?

Peace at Work

I don't have to be the one to tell you that life may not always look like we expected. Let's invite an aha moment right here: Today's trials really don't have to rob our peace. What if? What if God is using His piece of work in our lives to display His peace at work in our spirits?

It's just like God to use a mix of beauty and pain. And I certainly don't know what your idea of a beautiful moment looks like or what keeps you from a night's sleep and threatens to steal your peace. What I do know is this: We can see peace if we look for it. We can know peace if we know God.

When our fourteen-year old daughter was diagnosed with a brain tumor, I'm not going to lie, I tried, but I didn't have a good handle on peace. In fact, the first few nights in the hospital, I woke often from nightmares. Brittany would still be sleeping, her face tranquil. Her breath untroubled and rhythmic. I wondered how she slept through such a storm. I marveled and thanked God for her calm while the green recliner I tried to sleep in chomped down on me like a hungry alligator. But it wasn't the alligator I was wrestling with. Or my total lack of sleep. It was a total lack of peace. It seemed—to our unpleasant surprise—God had constructed something on purpose that looked like a complete accident. It wasn't. Twelve years later, we still marvel at the beautiful piece of work in Brittany's life. God's *peace* at work!

Perfect Peace

That's where we find hope, smack dab in the middle of this perfectly imperfect, alligator chomping, world. We find tranquility in the arms of a perfect God, because God is peace. His perspective is perfect. His eyes scan the tips of heaven and beyond.

> "So we fix our eyes not on what is seen, but on what is unseen, since what is seen is temporary, but what is unseen is eternal" (2 Corinthians 4:18 NIV).

It's tempting to fix our eyes on temporary flaws and glance over the grand landscape of forever. We see a job loss. A difficult marriage. A financial upset. A poor diagnosis. We see stressors and troubles and an unfinished hope of tomorrow. In her book, *Unglued* (Thomas Nelson, 2012), Lysa TerKeurst explains it this way, "Thinking on truth wraps our minds in a peace that rises above our circumstances." Take it from me, we can rise above and view beyond the surface of this rough, and sometimes splintered, life.

Although I've tried to avoid whatever pain might be coming next. You and I both know we can't. Life is messy—we have to make peace with that. There is no stepping over it. No walking around it. We've got to behold it and then walk with God through it...like walking through a doorway. A doorway with a big beautiful door. Hey, just like the lovely door to my office. Oh. Last week someone else was curious, "Are you done with this door?" Yes. We are done. Absolutely done. Beauty is *absolutely* in the eye of the barn door beholder.

Added Accents of Colorful Hope from Rhonda

I love the idea of a rough and unfinished door becoming a just-right entryway. Sometimes the roughest parts of life become the loveliest entries into the peaceful presence of the Father.

When it comes to those rough times, I really do want to remember Beth's this:

> Know my salvation.
>
> Know God doesn't leave me.
>
> Let His peace guard my mind and heart.

Lord, I ask that You would keep me alive and alert to the knowledge that You're working—and keep me reveling in the peace I can find in that knowing.

Fix Our Eyes on Him

"Finally, brothers, and sisters, whatever is true, whatever is noble, whatever is right, whatever is pure, whatever is lovely, whatever is admirable—if anything is excellent or praiseworthy—think about such things. Whatever you have learned or received or heard from me—put into practice. And the God of peace will be with you" (Philippians 4:8-9).

Bringing It Home

The filter of truth we can really count on to adjust our peace perspective is God's Word. Read and memorize these words of Jesus in John 16:33, "I have said these things to you, that in me you may have peace. In the world, you will have tribulation. But take heart; I have overcome the world." Let the words of Christ speak peace to you every time the Lord brings it to mind.

Look again at the last part of that verse. "But take heart; I have overcome...." Insert your trial right here. There is nothing in your life He can't overcome.

Read Philippians 4:5-6 again. What are the three commands given in this verse?

Have you ever felt God granted you a sense of calm while in prayer or worship? God is peace, so when we seek Him, we are, in essence, seeking peace. List three of your favorite verses that encourage you to trust the Lord for calm in the middle of the storm.

When we substitute peace for anxiety, we are better able to fix our eyes on the good and see beyond the storm. Philippians 4:8 gives us a list of things we can meditate on to find that peace, that sense of calm. "Whatever is true, whatever is honorable, whatever is just, whatever is pure, whatever is lovely, whatever is commendable, if there is any excellence, if there is anything worthy of praise, think about these things."

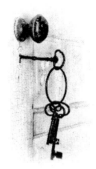

Chapter Eighteen

Fool-Proofing Life

Rhonda

I've come across a lot of projects and products labeled "idiot-proof"—building projects, craft projects—all kinds. As a matter of fact, I've tried some of those idiot-proof tech products myself, and do you know what I've found? Sometimes they grossly underestimate the power of a true tech-idiot. You have to be near genius level to even read the instructions on your average electronic device these days. And I'm talking about the instructions for the on/off switch. For a calculator. I heard somewhere that genius in all areas is 99% perspiration and 62% wishing you had listened in math class.

I would add a pithy phrase about a circumference here—if I had a little more math knowledge.

Still, while I may not have listened all that well in math class, anytime I'm talking about the maths and sciences that I know nothing about, I've started using lots more "air quotes." That way even if I'm saying something "stupid," I still look incredibly "clever."

Clever is as clever does (she said with flourishing finger quotes).

Doesn't it seem that our culture presents new, bizarre ideas every day about what it means to be clever and what it is to be knowledgeable? People say, "A little knowledge is a dangerous thing." But I was watching TV the other day, and it seems to me that a whole lot of foolishness is even more dangerous. A knowledgeable person, one who is knowledgeable in the things that really count, is a rare and wonderful find. Proverbs 20:15 backs me up on the point: "There is gold and a multitude of jewels, but knowledgeable lips are a rare treasure" (HCSB).

The Math and Science of Knowledge

So how do we find that rare treasure? Proverbs 2:1-6 says, "My son, if you accept my words and store up my commands within you, listening closely to wisdom and directing your heart to understanding; furthermore, if you call out to insight and lift your voice to understanding, if you seek it like silver and search for it like hidden treasure, then you will understand the fear of the LORD and discover the knowledge of God. For the LORD gives wisdom; and from His mouth come knowledge and understanding" (HCSB). Wisdom, knowledge, understanding—they're all from the Lord.

It's not, however, a passive pursuit. Our instructions in that Proverbs passage are especially verb-heavy. We're told to *accept* words, *store* commands, *listen* and *direct* our hearts. Then we're instructed to *call* out to insight and understanding, to *seek* and *search* for that kind of knowledge as we would *passionately hunt* for treasure. There's a hefty percentage of perspiration there. Accepting, storing, listening, directing, calling, seeking and searching leads to knowing Him more.

Reno projects can be verb-heavy for sure. Sanding, scraping, hammering—more. I would dare say, searching for knowledge and pursuing godly wisdom is heavier still, with so much weightier an influence on life.

Paul told the Christians in Colossae that he prayed this for them: "That you may be filled with the knowledge of His will in all wisdom and spiritual understanding, so that you may walk worthy of the Lord, fully pleasing to Him, bearing fruit in every good work and growing in the knowledge of God" (Colossians 1:9-10 HCSB).

The knowledge of His will results in *walking* worthy, *pleasing* Him, *doing* good works. More verbs! And these actions lead us to be—are you ready for this?—"growing in the knowledge of God." Full circle! It's like the most blessed circumference of knowledge. And it begins and ends with our powerful God. He is heavy, heavier, heaviest on the action. He will do all the "verbing" in and through us. Knowledge *is* power! But only His knowledge. And all by His power.

Knowledge or Wisdom? Let's Verb Them Both!

While we're talking about "heavy" and "verbing," it's always good to exercise some wisdom. I'll confess that when it comes to the physical—especially things physical and *fried*—I don't always exercise great wisdom.

"Exercise." "Extra fries." They sound a lot alike. So it's no wonder I keep getting them mixed up.

Maybe that could explain some of this weight gain. I'm not exactly saying I've *had* any weight gain, of course. I will admit, however, that when I weighed myself a couple of weeks ago, I found myself addressing the bathroom scale.

Okay, scale. Let's just agree to disagree.

Since the scale was being so judgmental, I decided to choose the salad instead of fries when we went out to dinner the next week. That one time I chose salad over fries, though, I stood up and shouted self-righteously to everyone in the crowded restaurant, "Health is a lifestyle choice, people!" Then I sat down. Then I ate somebody else's fries.

I didn't really stand and shout. But in my mind, I did. The rally cry was true. Health is a lifestyle choice. Sometimes, let me tell you simply, I make the wrong one.

Weighing In On Wisdom

There's a difference between knowledge and wisdom. And we really do need both. Knowledge? Yes! There are truths we are to learn and truly know. Wisdom, then, is the ability to turn that knowledge into yet more verbs—to turn it into God-powered right actions and all-around godly living.

We all make life choices every day. When we think about wise choices, weighing it out, as it were, sometimes we experience a different kind of a fight. An inner battle. Our flesh—that sinful bent inside us that wants to rule—battles for control. And it fights dirty.

The flesh whispers in my ear, telling me to listen to my gut, to trust my feelings. I say whisper, but it's more of a crowded restaurant kind of shout. Did I mention that my flesh is surprisingly strong and aggravatingly wily? Competitive too. It hates to lose.

So how do I battle this stubborn flesh and choose wisely instead? Truthfully, the battle isn't even mine. The battle is the Lord's and it's won as I trust in and surrender to Him. In every choice I make, I decide whether to give in to that flesh or to trust in the Lord, believe in and obey His word, submit to His Spirit who lives in me. His Holy Spirit provides all the strength I need to say no to my feelings and to say yes to His righteousness.

The Foolproof is in the Filling

Paul charges us in Ephesians 5:15 to "Pay careful attention, then, to how you walk—not as unwise people but as wise" (HCSB). Then he gives us the how-to in verse 18 when he follows it up with, "be filled with the Spirit." That's the DIY part—our part—being filled. Inviting the Spirit of God to take over and defeat the flesh.

We can trust Him to work in us to respond in wise obedience. And lest we get all weird and self-righteous about our wise choices and, I don't know, start yelling condescendingly in restaurants or something, it's good to focus in on the knowledge that it really is the Spirit of God who gives the wisdom. And it's He who provides the power to fight the flesh. He is the one who gives the strength to conquer flesh and choose well.

I wonder if there's anything that feels quite as good as trusting in Him to help us make good choices, idiot-proofing life, so to speak, and then seeing our lives take off in a healthier direction because of those wise choices.

I'm talking about the spiritual here, but it would no doubt do me some good to exercise a bit more wisdom on the physical side—maybe ease off the fries and go a little more enthusiastically in the salad direction. Because those scales? They also fight dirty. I may or may not be using finger quotes here.

Added Accents of Colorful Hope from Beth

I feel for Rhonda. Did you know a person can be required to make over a thousand decisions a day with 226.6 of those being food-related? It's not easy to make the wise choices. Wise renovating choices. Wise career choices. Or wise ministry choices. Many years ago, I prayerfully considered joining the P31 Ministries speaking team. Even though it was a huge ministry opportunity, I'd have missed countless football games, cross-country meets, and mounds and mounds of laundry. Most of all, I'd have missed time with my family. Believe me, prayer coupled with faith equals God's perfect wisdom and timing. My "not right now" back then has resulted in blessings all the way through. Mounds and mounds of blessing!

Fix Our Eyes on Him

> "For the Lord gives wisdom; from his mouth come knowledge and understanding; he stores up sound wisdom for the upright; he is a shield to those who walk in integrity, guarding the paths of justice and watching over the way of his saints. Then you will understand righteousness and justice and equity, every good path; for wisdom will come into your heart, and knowledge will be pleasant to your soul" (Proverbs 2:6-10).

Bringing It Home

Knowledge and wisdom overlap at times, but it's for sure we do well to actively seek both. List the action words again in that verb-packed passage, Proverbs 2:1-6. How can you actively seek? Write out an action you can take, personally, for each verb.

Name some ways you can stay proactive in ensuring you make wise choices every day.

What weapons—or tools—can you utilize when it comes to battling the flesh? If the old wallpaper in an home remodeling project is stubborn to let go, do we walk away and let it win? No. We pull out the best tools and tips available to us until that wallpaper is gone.

Look again at the Proverbs passage in the "Fix Our Eyes on Him" section. Underline each word that refers to an aspect of knowledge or wisdom. Let the first four words of that passage soak into your thinking and bring joy to your soul.

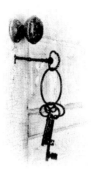

Chapter Nineteen

Tiny House, Big Love

Beth

"You sure haven't been yourself." My husband clicked on the turn signal as we headed to one of our daughter's last track meets of her high school career. Soon our baby would slip into her cap and gown. Brooklyn would flip her tassel and watch our home become a tiny spec in her rear-view mirror.

Jerry was right. I was a little out of sorts thinking about her leaving. A big, mom-baby, in fact—one who was having trouble letting go of a well-loved blanket—or more precisely, her babies.

There is a term that helps describe a large part of who I am. A word that's been spoken, yelled, sighed, moaned, sung, and cried out. Sometimes in surprise. Sometimes in pain. A palindrome that written backward or forward reads the same: Mom.

I've tried to stay conscious of being my own person over the years. But smooshy kisses and jelly-slathered fingers have tugged on my hands and on my heart. Talking with Jerry as we prepared to watch our daughter leave home, I was having trouble remembering who I was before my thoughts of "myself" got a little absorbed in page two of *Winnie The Pooh,* when Pooh lost his honey pot. Most likely I haven't had many uninterrupted thoughts since the kids. That's not so bad. So many of my own wants have fallen away and have been replaced with joy in and love for my children.

Little Box, Big Love

I pondered it all. A few days earlier, when I'd gone down to the basement to clean, I pulled out the brown shoe box marked "Fragile." Opening the box and gently peeling back the tissue paper, I found clay treasures there: a white owl, pink octopus, and a bowl molded from the young hands of one of my kids. Each with the inscription: "To: Mom."

I was amazed at how much love fit into that tiny box. Special gifts for an ordinary mom like me, though I had to laugh at the thought of "ordinary." Brooklyn and I had a conversation when she was four years old. In that conversation, she helped make my "ordinary"—just regular ol' me—feel special.

"Mommy. I decided something today. When I grow up, I want to be a regular mom, just like you."

"A *regular* mom?"

"Yeah. A mommy like you. Regular."

"What does a regular mom do, Honey?"

"Well, you do waundry, and make our peanut butter sandwiches. Kiss us. Help me read. Tell me to put on clean socks and stuff."

Her concept of who I was registered as just too delightfully enlightening. I had to know more.

"What's 'and stuff'?"

"Like eat chocolate all night with daddy after I go to bed."

"Honey, I don't eat chocolate *all* night," I corrected.

"Yeah-huh. I see wrappers."

So maybe we should've slept more and eaten chocolate less? Maybe *that's* why we felt completely exhausted some days. So funny! Chocolate or no, though, parenting can be tiring. Exhausting, really. Baseball games, cross-country meets, football games. And still, I'd do it all again in a heartbeat.

The time with my children had dashed by. I thought about how every second of being a parent was so worth the difficulty, exhaustion, and urgency. That's who I was, a busy mom in a rush who didn't mind being there for my kids. Did I take enough time in the urgency, however, to show my kids who I really am? A child of

God. Were they able to catch a small glimpse of God through all my mommy sacrifice?

Tiny Taste of Forever

That's what parents do—sacrifice. The greatest solitary sacrifice was from God. "For God so loved the world, that he gave his only Son, that whoever believes in him shall not perish but have eternal life" (John 3:16). God's willingness to sacrifice His only Son means we're loved in a way that can complete our identity. Not just as moms, wives, sisters, co-workers, or friends, but as His children.

Like a parent for a child, He is intent on meeting our needs according to His will and purposes. Scripture tells us someone brought children to Jesus. "Then children were brought to him that he might lay his hands on them and pray. The disciples rebuked the people, but Jesus said, 'Let the little children come to me, and do not hinder them, for to such belongs the kingdom of heaven'" (Mathew 19:14). Jesus wanted the children to come to Him to be nurtured and prayed for. He wants to nurture and provide for us, too—for all eternity. That's a large kind of love.

I have trouble understanding a love that big. God's love. I guess when I think of it in relation to the affection I have for my children, and then multiply it by infinity, it becomes a tiny bit clearer. "See what great love the Father has lavished on us, that we should be called the children of God! And that is what we are! The reason the world does not know us is that it did not know him" (1John 3:1 NIV). God doesn't have a tiny plan for our future. He has an eternal plan. His blueprint is not scribbled on a napkin. It's detailed, precise, and covers everything we need, and everything we are.

Seeing myself through the eyes of God is an endless answer to my identity. So, I'm not worried if I can't remember who I was before I bore the name "Mom." I know who I am. God's child. Oh…and yes, a regular mom, who still likes to stuff chocolate!

Added Accents of Colorful Hope from Rhonda

It's mindboggling how we love our babies. Yet Beth is so right on. Our love for our children doesn't even scratch the surface when it comes to God's humongous love for us, His children. It's the kind of love that chases away worry. "Casting all your cares [all your anxieties, all your worries, and all your concerns, once and for all] on Him, for He cares about you [with deepest affection, and watches over you very carefully]" (1 Peter 5:7 AMP). *OK, Lord. We're ready to cast. And ready to let that "casting" renovate and revive us in how we how we think about ourselves and our roles, how we love, and how we live—all of it.*

Fix Our Eyes on Him

"And I pray that you, being rooted and established in love, may have power, together with all the Lord's holy people, to grasp how wide and long and high and deep is the love of Christ, and to know this love that surpasses knowledge—that you may be filled to the measure of all the fullness of God" (Ephesians 3:17-19 NIV).

Bringing It Home

Look at Ephesians 3:17-19 from "Fix Our Eyes" again. Write it in your journal or on a notecard you can take with you. Let it be a reminder to you everywhere you go that you are deeply loved by a good Father.

Read Matthew 7:11, another glimpse into God's love for you. What does it reveal to us about His capacity to love?

We are called to love others. One of the best ways to love others is to go to God in prayer and petition for their needs. If the Lord has put a friend on your heart, perhaps a friend in desperate need of God's renovating touch, take time to pray right now.

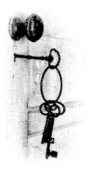

Chapter Twenty

Check the Toolbox for Brains and Grace

Rhonda

Tools. We've had some brain-talk in this section. Maybe it's because the brain is about the most useful tool we have when it comes to any kind of fixer upper. For some projects? It may also be one of the least used.

Have you heard it said that we humans only use 10% of our brains? Wait, what? That's a myth? I'm sad to hear that. Because I sort of liked the idea. I thought I could volunteer to be a case study for the research, even. Because I think most of the time I use much less than that.

On the other hand, it was frustrating to think about 90% of brain function remaining virtually untapped. What a waste. All those brain cells. Just sitting there with nothing to do.

I still get a little nervous about learning new things. Mostly because I figure "percentages" may not be my biggest obstacle. *Whatever* percent is in use, I only have a certain number of brain cells. It's a limited supply, I tell you. The little rascals are already occupied with keeping my heart beating, inhaling and exhaling, blinking, drinking coffee—all those basic, involuntary life functions. That has to consume 95% of my total brain function, right? So if I try to stuff new knowledge requiring more than my 5% leftover space, couldn't that squeeze out something else I've already learned? Maybe something I really need to know? What if I watch "Jeopardy" and accidentally learn way too much about the Articles of Confederation and then forget how to "math"—the verb. I'd hate to suddenly find I couldn't chemistry like I once could…chemistry.

Anybody Following the Math Here?

Okay yes, I do know I could never really…math. And I've certainly never been able to…chemistry. But I never know how my brain is going to mess with me. I can't count how many times I've sat at the computer with a pressing writing deadline, telling my brain, "Let's go, buddy. Gotta get in gear." Then, just to be funny, my brain will send me into a nonstop loop of "Grandma Got Run Over by a Reindeer." In those moments, my brain will bring to mind every word of that song. No other words of any kind. Just those.

The human brain. What an interesting mystery. It was designed by an infinite God of boundless creative power. Imagine *His* brain! His thinking power is too amazing for our little brains to process. It's a true mind-boggle. He tells us in Isaiah 55, "For My thoughts are not your thoughts… For as heaven is higher than earth, so My ways are higher than your ways and My thoughts than your thoughts" (vs. 9 HCSB).

In focusing on the God of infinite knowledge and wisdom we find peace of mind—our own brain-peace. "You keep him in perfect peace, whose mind is stayed on You, because he trusts in You" (Isaiah 26:3 NKJV). This brain of mine can be like an untrained puppy. And sometimes making peace with it becomes a matter of tugging on the leash to "sit" and "stay."

A mind stayed on Him—there's my brain's sweet spot. All my mind, all my heart, all my strength, all my soul—all!

Meanwhile, I'm ever so thankful for His loving patience with beings of finite mind. Sometimes I still find it challenging to keep my brain cells all firing in the same direction for any length of time without getting distracted. Have I mentioned that my brain may have its work cut out for it? Because sometimes the ADD kicks in and those brain cells…how do you like my hair?

DIY, ADD and the Perfect Segue

I'm not sure which part of my brain or personality makes me the high-maintenance chick I am. Recently, though, I did at least shoot for being a little lower maintenance in the budget department. Like maybe becoming a bit more DIY in a few areas. You probably know me well enough by now to understand that do-it-yourself is rather out of my wheelhouse. I'm a lot more comfortable as a "do-it-for-me" kind of gal. But I was willing to try.

I decided to focus on the hair budget. No, not giving up the color. I'd dye first (pa-dum-ching). I don't think I'll ever be so low maintenance that I'll go colorless. But I thought surely I could color it myself. What could go wrong?

Oh my. Somehow, somewhere between the shake-this, the apply-that and the rinse-the-rest, I managed some sort of slinging spill—a gazillion splotches of hair color in all sizes and shapes, all over the carpet. And did I notice I'd done it so I could clean it right up? Oh no. I had to wait the half-hour it takes to permanently become one with the carpet. Most. Expensive. Hair color. Ever.

I told my husband, head hanging and shame-faced, that I'd made a major accidental art project of our carpet. He answered, "That's okay. It could've happened to me."

Could've happened to him? What, when he colored his hair? He doesn't have to color his hair. He doesn't have hair. But I'll tell you what he does have—grace. And lots of it.

Grace to Dye For

I thought about adding more dye splotches on the rest of the carpet in the splotched area. Because…leopard print! And though I still may put that DIY leopard rug idea on Pinterest, I decided against DIY-ing mine because, while my husband is full of grace, he's not much of a leopard-print-carpet kind of guy. It's good to know the grace is there if I need it though.

My hubby is full of grace because he's so full of Jesus. I love how he demonstrates the grace of God.

It's amazing to me that despite how messy my life gets—however much of my brain I engage to do it, and whatever stains I may slop and in whatever direction—God's grace is there. Unchanging. Steady. Always enough.

It's God's grace that saves us. Paul says in Ephesians 2:8, "For you are saved by grace through faith, and this is not from yourselves; it is God's gift" (HCSB).

And it's God's grace that sustains us. When Paul was experiencing pain, the Lord told him, "My grace is sufficient for you" (2 Corinthians 12:9 HCSB). For every difficulty we face, His oh-so-sufficient grace is waiting. It's the kind of grace that holds us up when circumstances threaten to flatten us and life seems all too difficult. In every one of those circumstances, by His grace, He offers us absolutely everything we really need.

Sufficient–Then More!

His grace is sufficient to save, sufficient to comfort, and sufficient to grow us into the faithful followers of Christ we long to be. And when we think we've seen all the grace there is, guess what. There's more! Grace after grace. "Indeed, we have all received grace after grace from His fullness" (John 1:16 HCSB).

Brains and grace. It actually makes sense that we would have them sitting right next to each other in our "life renovation toolbox," as you might call it, while we're learning to allow the Father to revive our perspective.

O Lord, let my mind be stayed on You! All my heart, all my strength, all my soul, and, yes, 100% of my mind. Thank You, Lord, for your grace that cleans my every splotchy life-mess. And thank You for the "more" grace You give even after that.

Color me grateful for the way He changes our lives, and the way He continues to mold and revive our perspective through it all as well. Color me grateful all the way to the roots even. That's enough chemistry for me.

Added Accents of Colorful Hope from Beth

Speaking of the mind, my husband's mind is pretty sharp. Not only is he wise, but he sets his mind on becoming more like Christ. He renews his attention in God's Word, and he revives his awareness of others through prayer. He is definitely more about doing than he is about saying. Me? I tend to be much more about saying. Just saying. And although it goes without saying—but I have to say it, I'm so very thankful for Jerry's generous grace. Very, very, very thankful.

Fix Our Eyes on Him

> "But grow in the grace and knowledge of our Lord and Savior Jesus Christ. To him be the glory both now and to the day of eternity. Amen" (2 Peter 3:18).

Bringing It Home:

It's good to remember that God thinks so much bigger than we do (Isaiah 55:8-9). How does dwelling on that put us at ease? How does Isaiah 26:3 fit into this line of thinking?

Does your brain ever lead you astray, taking you down a neuro-path that goes nowhere? What do you do to refocus those rogue thoughts?

How do you see "brains and grace" fitting together in our life remodel toolbox? How can this kind of thinking mold and remake our perspective?

If you haven't yet, pray the prayer at the end of this chapter that begins with "O Lord, let my mind be stayed on You!" Write it on a piece of paper and put it next to your bed. Would you be willing to pray this prayer first thing in the morning for a week? Talk about a perspective-changer!

Part *Six*

Renew!

Chapter Twenty-One

Fixer-Upper-Neighbor-Loving

Rhonda

I'm glad I confessed from the get-go that I'm a fixer upper. That perfectly-dressed gal sitting perfectly pretty in her perfectly-decorated home. You can be perfectly sure she's so not me.

People often ask what it was like when my kids were teens and pre-teens. When you have five kids in seven years, that means they're all rather teen-ish at the same time. When people ask that question, I tell them it was basically about a ten-year search for somebody's missing shoe, plus seven-thousand school fundraisers. And also a whole lot of sweeping up breakfast cereal. Some of it from under the kids' beds.

Semi-interesting factoid: "Total" is a relatively healthy breakfast cereal, I hear. But not when it's been left under the bed with dirty sweat socks. For two weeks. It transforms into something else. Even if I could describe it, you wouldn't want me to.

During the years of so many teens in the house, I do wonder exactly how many times I had to say things like, "Son. You have to clean your room. We're out of spoons." I remember sweeping the kitchen floor, wondering how it was possible that I could sweep up more breakfast cereal than I'd purchased. Ever.

It also amazed me that the kids never noticed any of it. They could walk across the kitchen floor, crunching from one side to the other, with nary a blink. How? You'd think the vibrations alone would make them look down. Though it didn't matter because even if they did cast a downward glance, they *still* never saw the cereal.

How Could You Not Notice?

I would make fun of them a little more if I didn't all too often struggle with my own blind spots. I'd so much rather find fault in someone else than recognize any crunch of my own. I'll admit it straight out. I can hear your crunch from a couple of miles away while not even seeing the houseful of Fruit-Loop-dust I'm standing in.

But Jesus helps us see differently, not so quickly dismissing our own snaps, crackles, and pops. In Matthew 7:3, He asked, "Why do you see the speck that is in your brother's eye, but do not notice the log that is in your own eye?" It would be comical if it weren't so sad. And so true. Here I stand pointing out someone else's tiny corn pop while I'm neck-deep in my own?

Jesus went on, "Or how can you say to your brother, 'Let me take the speck out of your eye,' when there is the log in your own eye? You hypocrite, first take the log out of your own eye, and then you will see clearly to take the speck out of your brother's eye" (Matthew 7:4-5).

Every time we allow Jesus to help us see as He does, all those hypocrisies are swept out. His are eyes of love. We're told in the "love is" list in 1 Corinthians 13 that "Love finds no joy in unrighteousness but rejoices in the truth. It bears all things, believes all things, hopes all things, endures all things" (vv. 6-7 HCSB).

Eyes of love are truthful. They're not hypocritical. There's no self-seeking there. They help us not perceive ourselves as better than the next person. Paul made it clear in Romans 12:9 when he said that "love must be without hypocrisy," and a few verses earlier, "I tell everyone among you not to think of himself more highly than he should think" (Romans 12:3 HCSB).

Jesus-vision brings a total transformation in how we think of ourselves, and how we think of and respond to others. *Total* transformation. Which this time is not even a remote cereal reference.

Off the Shelf and By the Book

Anytime we're moving from cereal dust to just plain…dust-dust, I don't mind reminding you that I'm a fixer upper. My favorite part of dusting the bookshelves in my office, for instance, is the part where I never really do it. At all. And actually, it's my personal belief that if you can see dust on a bookshelf, that means there aren't enough books on it.

Incidentally, I'm always on the lookout for more books. And for more reasons than to buy more books. Okay, yes, I may have a bit of a book problem. Some may think me "shelf-ish" (I know, I can't believe I said it either). I think I'd rather call it a dust problem, but whatever.

My favorite way to dust the bookshelves? Turn on the ceiling fan. After a few swirls of the fan, the dusting is done and I can sit down and read a book.

I won't deny that I do have a lot of shelves—with a lot of books protecting all those shelves from dust. I was standing in the doorway staring into my office the other day and suddenly found myself thinking it's a little embarrassing that though I have so many shelves and so many books, there's not a book in there anywhere that I can pull to open a secret passage. What an unfortunate oversight when we built the room.

Not Exactly a Secret

Neglected secret passages aside, there are oversights along this life journey that are so much more unfortunate. I wish I could tell you that I've never overlooked a person. I would love to tell you I've never neglected giving needed attention to the people I'm called to love. But I have.

Does it ever happen to you? You see someone across the room and avoid eye contact so the person doesn't mistakenly feel welcomed into a conversation. Or you're at the grocery store and quickly jerk your cart onto an aisle you don't need to visit, all to dodge getting trapped into a dialogue with that guy from down the street.

I need to regularly dust off my compassion and grace and become intentional in the way I love. Active love doesn't avoid. As a matter of fact, it purposefully searches out opportunities to love—even to love the unlovely. To love the annoying. The foolish. The depressing.

The smelly. The inconvenient people. An active love, dusted off and in use, is a love that goes yet beyond that. A God kind of love *runs* to meet those people.

It's no secret that we can love like that as we allow the God of love to do it in us. "Beloved, let us love one another, for love is from God, and whoever loves has been born of God and knows God. Anyone who does not love does not know God, because God is love" (1 John 4:7-8).

To love unselfishly is to allow the God who *is* love to work in us. Anytime we're not loving others, we're testifying to the world that the Gospel hasn't changed us on the inside as we claim. It's like shelving our Gospel effectiveness.

Our love for others is our testimony. We're the book others read, as it were. "By this all people will know that you are My disciples, if you have love for one another" (John 13:35 HCSB).

O Lord, may we be quick to love the unloveliest. As You work Your love in and through our lives, may we ever love like You.

Here's hoping we're on the same page. Me? I'm mostly an open book. A fixer upper. But mostly an open book.

Added Accents of Colorful Hope from Beth

I want to refute the myth that says you have to be altogether perfect to walk into a church. I walked in one Sunday with giant size-stickers still pasted on both the front and the back of my new slacks. No one there could've missed the fact that I was a size "medium." "M – M – M – M." A kind lady noticed the sticker on front. She was looking for volunteers for the children's ministry. She did not ask me. Later, my daughter noticed the sticker on the back of my pants. My family now always does a sticker-check on me before I leave the house. Without judging. *Lord, keep me from judging and not loving. Help me first to see the 20-foot plank in my eye, and impart the ever-present need of You humbly before me, and also, behind me. Amen.*

Fix Our Eyes on Him

"A new commandment I give to you, that you love one another: just as I have loved you, you also are to love one another. By this all people will know that you are my disciples, if you have love for one another" (John 13:34-35).

Bringing It Home

Blind spots. By definition, we can't see our own. We're blind to them. But it's true that "Jesus helps us see differently." Has He ever revealed a blind spot to you, especially where it concerned how you love others?

Look at the entire love chapter, 1 Corinthians 13. Are there any in that list of characteristics that are not as evident in your life as the others? What do you suppose it takes to strengthen the weak areas? In our renovation terminology, what needs reinforcing? What do you do when you find someone is difficult to love?

Have you ever searched someone out to show them love? Is there something you've done in the past that surprised you in the way it made someone else feel special and loved? How can you continue, and even build on, the ways the Lord loves people through you? How can you allow the God who *is* love to love others through you even more? Practically speaking, what might that look like?

Chapter Twenty-Two

Flip or Flop–And Flip-Flops

Beth

I usually don't consider walking a dog a challenge. But then, that was before Wesson.

When we picked our yellow lab puppy out of a litter of nine, the kids noticed his fur was the color of the sun. His face seemed to say, "Own me. I am a sleepy, sunshine puppy." I pictured long, serene, and leisurely strolls in the park. The puppy even gave a peaceful yawn as we watched him "watch" the other dogs.

"Perfect. We'll take him." That was the last time he yawned. Pleasant puppy ownership was replaced with hyper and jumping and all-things-chewing. Chewing the leather strap right off my favorite purse, among the list of lost.

A few months later, I took the overactive little purse-chewer for a walk. He had put on an impressive amount of muscle in those previous weeks so I had to work to keep him in tow. Then the neighbor's dog came out and offered a little puppy visit. To say Wesson responded enthusiastically is an outrageous understatement. The greeting was more than he could resist. He put into action more muscle than I knew he had as he took off in a whole-hearted launch.

He bolted. I flipped. I soared, really. Vertically, but with some height. I must've been airborne for only a few seconds, but it felt like more. Still, I was *not* letting go of that leash. I didn't land until Wesson came to abrupt halt. That's when I flopped right onto my shoulder. It was the most unpleasant flip-flop I'd ever pulled off. How ironic that I was wearing flip-flops. And I might've laughed if I hadn't been in some serious pain. It was my aerial flip-flop that later landed me in the office of an orthopedic surgeon. Dr. Bernhard said he'd seen injuries like mine before. "You have what looks like a severe football-type injury." OK, even with the pain, I had to laugh at that.

My kids later commented that I was brave for not letting go of the leash. Hmmm. It hadn't occurred to me to let go. Bravery. Yeah, let's call it that.

Fixer-Committed

A commitment to something or someone can be a not-letting-go proposition as well. Maybe it shouldn't occur to us that letting go is even an option. It does take work. But the rewards can be awesome. Even fun.

Like the fixer-upper Jerry and I bought in our first year of marriage. It was the worst house on the nicest block. We knew it had potential, though. All it needed was some love and attention. High maintenance attention, actually. I've already confessed to being a fix-her-upper wife. That first year, I was about as drippy and demanding as the leaky roof. Poor Jerry. Married a fixer-upper. Bought another fixer-upper. Maybe more "fun" than any one man could handle.

The tub faucet in our fixer-upper not only leaked, but it would also give a random electrical shock whenever it felt like it. I may be a fixer-upper but at least I hardly ever do that. Apparently, our bodies would act as a "ground" and we got that zap when we touched the tub faucet while standing on the floor. We were surprised—no, *shocked*—when we discovered just how much work that house really needed.

One good surprise, though, was the neighborhood. We met Lowell and Barb from across the street. It wasn't long before they felt so much more like family than neighbors. They invested in us at least as much as we invested in that house. Maybe more. As they saw us pouring our time and energy and money into our costly porch, expensive roof, and high dollar siding, they gave us some great advice. Free! Never assume your marriage will maintain itself.

They gave us a gift, as well, in allowing us to observe the way they loved each other and how they loved God more. Lowell and Barbara Kline exemplified what it was to love the Lord with everything they had. Heart, mind, and soul. And they encouraged us to live that way too.

It's not simply a neighborly suggestion in Scripture. It's a commandment given by Jesus. "'Love the Lord your God with all your heart and with all your soul and with all your mind.' This commandment is the first and greatest commandment" (Matthew 22:38 NIV).

Honoring God with heart, soul, and mind is the least we can do when we consider His steadfast love and His firm commitment to us. "The steadfast love of the Lord never ceases; his mercies never come to an end; they are new every morning; great is your faithfulness." (Lamentations 3:22-23).

He doesn't let go. God's love meets every need. His is a soul-renewing, never-fainting love, a lifeline we can hold onto forever.

Hang On to This

Not only is God's love a steadfast love, it's also a love that withstands all. Take a look at how enduring it is: "Give thanks to the Lord, for he is good, for his steadfast love endures forever. Give thanks to the god of Gods, for his steadfast love endures forever. Give thanks to the Lord of lords, for his steadfast love endures forever" (Psalm 136:1-3).

There is no one—not parents or family or neighbors or even spouses—who can outlast or out-stay or out-love God. And the more we love the Lord, the greater our capacity to love others in return.

Jerry and I are so blessed. Thirty years together and we know we couldn't have done it without the enduring love of God. Through Him we've discovered a renewed spirit. We've experienced renewed faith and a renewed commitment to that faith. We know that marriage can be a walk in the park. A wonderful, wild, and sometimes very eventful walk. I'm praying we'll always be brave.

Lord, I am praying Your love continues to reach out and renew our hearts. Give us the ability to trust in Your undeniable affection for us. If we are walking in a marriage that seems without love, without hope, or without the firm foundation of Your love, we ask You to rescue, even now. Grant the strength to hold on. For the one who feels lonely and unloved, I ask You to fill every empty part with Your Spirit. All because of Jesus, Amen.

Added Accents of Colorful Hope from Rhonda

Lu Lu is the little dog who rules our house. We don't even pretend she doesn't anymore. She knows it. We know it. We're all accepting her rule and moving on from here. The funny thing is that this Pekinese/poodle/Chihuahua mix weighs about seven pounds. She rules by sass-power alone. She's got the tude, but if she ever has to defend her right to reign, I wonder what she'll use for the brawn part.

Our heavenly Father? He defends His right to rule with all of history. And with all of creation. And with all the power of the entire universe. I'm praising Him today for His power—and for His ever-mystifying, glorious, steadfast love. So steadfast. "Dogged," you might say.

Incidentally, I'm mystified in a totally different way when it comes to my dog. Still scratching my head. Because what even *is* a peeka-poo-huahua?

Fix Our Eyes on Him

"Oh give thanks to the Lord, for he is good, for his steadfast love endures forever! Let the redeemed of the Lord say so, whom he has redeemed from trouble and gathered in from the lands, from the east and from the west, from the north and from the south.

Some wandered in desert wastes, finding no way to a city to dwell in; hungry and thirsty, their soul fainted within them. Then they cried to the Lord in their trouble, and he delivered them from their distress. He led them by a straight way till they reached a city to dwell in. Let them thank the lord for his steadfast love, for his wondrous works to the children of man!" (Psalm 107:2-8).

Bringing It Home:

In the previous chapter, we looked at 1 Corinthians 13. Check it out again. Look at verses 4-8. What are the true qualities of love that these verses speak to? How does looking at them again inspire you in your marriage? In other relationships? In your relationship with the Lord?

Think for a moment. What are some of the specific benefits of staying solidly anchored to God's steadfast love?

Look up Psalm 136:1-16. What does God want us to know about His eternal love? Is there any verse that jumps out—something that will fill a need or answer a question you have about love?

Take some time to thank the Lord for His enduring and undeniable love for you. "Give thanks to the Lord, for he is good, for his steadfast love endures forever" (Psalm 136:1).

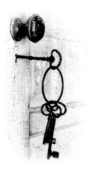

Chapter Twenty-Three

Hang On to Your Hardhat

Rhonda

If hanging onto reality is anything like hanging pictures, mine probably needs to go a little higher and to the right.

I know, I know. There are all kinds of tools and methods to make picture-hanging easier. But I think I only feel I've put in the right amount of energy when I'm left with four or five holes for every one nail. I'm surprised they don't make me get a permit. Or wear a hard hat.

Tap in a nail. Hang the picture. Eyeball it. Take down the picture. Pull out the nail. Put the nail closer to the right spot. Tap it in. Hang the picture. Eyeball it. Repeat as needed. That's my system.

In the end, if at least one of the holes in the wall is closer to the size of the hammer head than the nail, *that's* when I feel I might've put enough heart in it. Annnnd, welcome to my reality.

I do know if I tried levels and measuring tools and put some of that math and science into it that we talked about in earlier chapters, I could probably save my walls from the severe Swiss-cheesing I've inflicted on them. But then what would I do with my hit and miss (more miss) system? Besides, I always buy extra wall décor and put it away in my "for covering accidental holes" stash. The wall where I had that solo wall piece in mind? It now holds my favorite grouping. Hello, collage!

Did I mention how grateful I am for a husband who is very patient? Also one who knows drywall repair?

Patiently Hanging on Every Word

Patience is not just a tool we pick up in a moment we think we might happen to need it. That's "real" reality. Patience is one of the things we're told to "wear." We don't just hang it on the wall. We hang it upon our person—inside our character.

When Paul issues the charge in Colossians 3:12 to "clothe yourselves with compassion, kindness, humility, gentleness and patience" (NIV), he's giving us quite a wonderful collage of character qualities. This is without a doubt a high and lovely grouping!

Hanging onto the first four can tack the patience right alongside. Just try to be impatient when you're wearing compassion. Nope, not happening. Let the impatience fly at the same time you're walking in the kindness of the Lord. Can't happen. Put on impatience and humility at the same time? Can't manage that one either.

We deal with people every day who test our patience—people who are difficult, troubled, undisciplined, mean, lazy or just plain annoying. If I try for a second to offer them patience from my own personal supply, it's not even going to be hit and miss. It's more likely to be miss and miss some more. Godly patience only happens as we walk in the Spirit. That's why patience is included in the fruit of the Spirit list in Galatians 5:22-23. It's only through Him. He'll continue to bring us a little higher and to the right, so to speak, as we surrender to His leading.

And then? We can totally *nail* this. Even when relationships are a bit, shall we say, "squeezy"?

The Big Squeeze

Our Sammy-cat understands "squeezy" from a couple of directions. According to Sammy, there's no container that's not worth sitting in. If there's a bag, box, bowl, bin, basin, or bucket he can reach, there's an understood "Dibs!" from Sammy as he slowly fills the container with himself. I had a rectangular basket sitting out the other day and Sammy poured himself inside it—well, poured *most* of himself inside it—and when I looked over, all I could see was a loaf of Sammy. A loaf! It was so weird.

Sammy has a thing about his personal space. Never mind the fact that he'll give it up completely for any strange vessel. We're all still supposed to know never to invade Sammy's personal space.

Then there's the LuLu-pup. She welcomes herself into everyone's space. Plus, she could easily be the perfect poster pup for canine ADHD. Sammy's worst nightmare. Just a bit ago she climbed into a chair, right up in Sammy's cat-grill. Sammy long ago perfected the facial expression of utter disgust. It's full-on right now. They're like two pods in a pea.

The funny thing is, LuLu doesn't even know that. She seems convinced they're best friends. How many times has she taken her ball and dropped it in front of Sammy? She waits expectantly every time. It doesn't matter how many times I say to her, "LuLu, seriously. When has Sammy ever played ball with you? *Ever?*"

As followers of Christ, though, it no doubt pleases our heavenly Father when we're a little less "Sammy" and a little more "LuLu." In some ways, anyway. It's good when we stop worrying and stewing about our own personal space, can that look of disgust, get out of our comfort zones and get to work for the Kingdom.

Two Pods in a Pea—But Loving Anyway

There's too much at stake to get sidetracked by personality differences or petty aggravations. Fighting like cats and dogs? It should never happen. Paul said in Philippians 1:27, "Just one thing: Live your life in a manner worthy of the gospel of Christ. Then, whether I come and see you or am absent, I will hear about you that you are standing firm in one spirit, with one mind, working side by side for the faith that comes from the gospel" (HCSB).

No "loafing"—let's live worthy of this gospel and work side by side for the faith. No fussing. No fur flying. Loving each other and loving a lost world into the Kingdom.

Is it easy to love people who are getting on your last nerve? Sammy would answer with a hiss. I, too, freely admit that not only isn't it easy, it's downright impossible. The moment we recognize we can't do it and we begin to depend solely on the God who can, that's the moment love happens in a new way. Because the Lord Himself is the one who makes it happen. "If anyone serves, it should be from the strength God provides, so that God may be glorified through Jesus Christ in everything" (1 Peter 4:11 HCSB).

What has to change within us so we'll "serve from the strength God provides"? What walls will He need to reframe? What flooring needs to be addressed, refinished, replaced?

It's crystal clear in 1 John 4:7, "Let us love one another, because love is from God." And that makes it right—and safe—for me to welcome you into my personal space. You're even welcome to help me hang pictures. Keep in mind you might need a hardhat.

Added Accents of Colorful Hope from Beth

My friends have practiced a ton of patience with me over the decades. Patience times about 250 pages during this book project, even. Patsy and Dana didn't complain the other day at lunch when I mumbled several sleep-deprived statements about shiplap and being up late to meet the book deadline and I don't even know what else. I do remember sleep-drooling into my tea. Tolerant friends.

When I take a moment to consider my failings, though, my battle with sin—sometimes the same sin over and over—I just cry. He's patient, my Jesus. Perfect love drives Him to wait it out. Even if it takes forever!

Fix Our Eyes on Him

"Love endures with patience and serenity, love is kind and thoughtful, and is not jealous or envious; love does not brag and is not proud or arrogant. It is not rude; it is not self-seeking, it is not provoked [nor overly sensitive and easily angered]; it does not take into account a wrong endured. It does not rejoice at injustice, but rejoices with the truth [when right and truth prevail]. Love bears all things [regardless of what comes], believes all things [looking for the best in each one], hopes all things [remaining steadfast during difficult times], endures all things [without weakening]. Love never fails [it never fades nor ends]" (1 Corinthians 13:4-8 AMP).

Bringing It Home

Write out Colossians 3:12 and read it every morning for a couple of weeks. "Get dressed" spiritually before going about your day. How do you think wearing compassion, kindness, humility, gentleness and patience might change how your day goes?

When we talk about people who test our patience, does a face immediately pop into your mind? Pray that the Holy Spirit will fill you with His patience in ways you've never even seen happen in your life before. Are you willing to ask Him to love and bless this person through you?

If there's someone who is especially challenging to love— someone you really don't feel like serving—try writing that person's name on a card. Write out 1 Peter 4:11 on that card, too, and make it a part of your prayer time with the Lord until you're confident God has done His kind of amazing work in that situation. What a great reminder that the strength is His, and the glory is His: "If anyone serves, it should be from the strength God provides, so that God may be glorified through Jesus Christ in everything" (1 Peter 4:11 HCSB).

Chapter Twenty-Four

If These Walls Could Talk

Beth

I was rolling yet another coat of paint on the living room walls when I started to wonder what these walls would say if they could talk. Well, besides, "This is like the fifth different color in the past two years, lady. Make up your mind already." I hope they wouldn't notice that the "Bahama Buff" I was layering on is also the same color from five favorites and two years ago. They may even argue with me about color choice.

I might not want to know everything those walls might say. They've seen some things. Like the times I slept through my turn at the tooth fairy run. Or even more personal, times when I made bigger mistakes. Times my impatience won out on long, hard days. Times I focused too long and hard on my need to be perfect.

I do hope the walls wouldn't be too judgmental. I hope they would've noticed the laughter and fun that's gone on inside and outside these two by fours. And while there were imperfections and times of impatience and days when I was anything but perfect, this home is also a place of warmth and caring. It's a home where there's been laughter until tears and tears until prayer. And I'm thankful we've kept the doors wide open to invite in family—and friends who've become like family. I'm thankful for God's graciousness in giving us good friends.

I've always made an eager, anxious pursuit of friendships outside these four walls. When it comes to fighting the hard battles of real life, friends can be lifesavers. True, some of us need more saving than others. This high-drama mama? I need a person who knows me. Who but a friend, for instance, would rescue me from a rogue nursing pad disaster? It took a true buddy to discretely scoop it up from the middle of a circle of adults in conversation. Stepped on top of it, then swooped down and snatched it up—all to save me from heavy-duty embarrassment. That's a friend.

Friends have a way of overlooking some of the "messy" in our lives, even seeing some of that messy as another opportunity to pray hard. The "step, swoop, and snatch" move is great, but there's something extra special about knowing someone is praying hard. It's a renewing breath of fresh air.

When Our Back's Against the Wall

We women need the renewing refreshment of friends. Sometimes the problems we're obliged to address and all the snap decisions we have to make in a day are overwhelming. A lunch and some chocolate and some conversation—there can be strength waiting for us right there.

Much more can be accomplished when we join together and head His direction. Let's look at this illustration in Scripture: "Again, I say to you, if two of you agree on earth about anything they ask, it will be done for them by my Father in heaven. For where two or three are gathered in my name, there am I among them." (Matthew 18:19-20). There is strength for our battles when we gather together. Battles of exhaustion, a hurting heart or even just the "am I really fixing meatloaf again?" battle.

Ecclesiastes 4:12 reminds us that we need each other in the battles. "And though a man might prevail against one who is alone, two will withstand him—a threefold cord is not easily broken."

Support Walls

When Mary, the mother of Jesus, was first pregnant, she headed with "haste" to see Elizabeth. Not only was Elizabeth also miraculously pregnant, but Elizabeth was there to encourage Mary. She said, "'Blessed are you among women, and blessed is the fruit of your womb!'" (Luke 1:42). Even Mary, Jesus' mother, needed a friend and kind words of inspiration and support. Elizabeth was Mary's cousin, but evidently she was also one of her confidants. God doesn't expect us to always go it alone. In relationships, He often makes us more aware of His work in us and around us.

The right kind of peer pressure can be a great asset in matters of faith. I went on a mission trip a few years ago, but not before being cheered by my best friend, Patsy, to forget my fear and forget foreign country spiders and seek the blessing. I have to say, it was a trip that had plenty of both—fear and furry spiders. And the fear of furry spiders. But I also found great blessing in sharing Christ and the blessing of making new friends. The Lord knows when we need someone to push us gently outside our comfort zone. And time zone. He reminds us how to lovingly encourage. "And let us consider how to stir up one another to love and good works, not neglecting to meet together, as is the habit of some, but encouraging one another, and all the more as you see the Day drawing near" (Hebrews 10:24, 25). Renewal happens right there.

Never Walling Ourselves Off

Relationships outside our four walls can stir us and spur us to His purposes in our lives. Ten years ago I initiated a friendship with Rhonda Rhea, for example. God grew our friendship through a shared love for ministry and writing. He had a plan to use us and our friendship, and He had a plan for this fix-her-upper ministry. You never know how God is going to work His good purposes through a friend.

Recently I read about the little Italian village of Acciaroli, where nearly 300 people are over 100 years of age. One hundred years old! Great genes, I'm sure. Plus a healthy, basil-rich diet. Those are probably contributing factors. But the people in the village are all very interconnected. Researchers speculate that the strong friendships they have and their strong habit of gathering frequently for laughter, food, and friendship is a key to their longevity. Friendships—they're healthy!

Our ultimate, best, most all-inclusive friendship will always be with the One who renews us, encourages us, and gives us hope in this life. Loving others, my family, my church and my friends is one way

I can demonstrate my love for Him. Still, my relationship with God is my number one priority.

Added Accents of Colorful Hope from Rhonda

I'm thankful for friends who have an especially high "drive you up the wall" threshold. I try to be a low-maintenance friend. I really do. But I've found that being low-maintenance is not exactly my strongest suit. I need the kind of friend who'll tell me to calm down now and again. One who'll tell me I should wear a jacket with that outfit. One who speaks the truth in love, even when the truth might be difficult to hear. Proverbs 27:6 says, "Faithful are the wounds of a friend." Truthful, loving friends are a sweet treasure. Particularly for those of us who are, shall we say, a little off the wall.

Fix Our Eyes on Him

"This is my commandment, that you love one another as I have loved you. Greater love has no man than this, that someone lay down his life for his friends. You are my friends if you do what I command you." (John 15: 12-14).

Bringing It Home

Friendships are vital, it's true. But they can never replace our need for a deep, deep relationship with God. What is your favorite Scripture passage that reminds you most of this need for relationship with your Creator?

Take time to update the part of your prayer list where you keep up with the needs of your friends. Who is God calling you to pray for today?

If you don't have a friend who you can be accountable to and who is accountable to you in spiritual things, ask the Lord to bring that person into your life. Start the process of initiating the relationship this very week.

Part *Seven*

Reclaim!

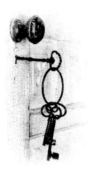

Chapter Twenty-Five

Open Concept

Beth

Some people can pull off "ordinary" without a hitch. By ordinary, I mean that they don't seem to turn everyday happenings into big, bizarre incidents. I admire those people. If only I knew how to be one of them.

I think one of the reasons I'm not one of those beautifully ordinary people is my penchant for thinking I need to take control. It's one of the reasons I coined the term "fix-her-upper" for myself several years ago. I definitely need some fixing in the control department. I'm telling you, I can make one of those big, bizarre incidents happen in the most innocuous places. Even a car wash.

I proved that one. We had just purchased a new-to-us car the day before when I decided to welcome it to the family with a super wash. I even paid the extra few bucks for the undercarriage wash. Hot wax? Don't mind if I do, thanks. That car was going to sparkle and shine, upside, sideways, underside, and every which-way.

I totally had this car wash thing. Left wheel aligned in the track? Check. Car in neutral? Yes. Headlights on? Yes. Windows rolled up? Yes and yes. The presoak solution was drizzling its way around the car when I noticed a little drip coming from the sunroof. Oops, might've forgotten to tighten that sunroof when I checked the other windows.

I fumbled hurriedly with the buttons. The first one? That was a no. Second one? Definitely not. The sun-roof opened even wider. I didn't get to try the third button before, oh my goodness, the high-powered jets exploded into action! Niagara! On my head!

Oh, My Soul–Losing Control

In an instant, I was blinking through rivulets of mascara—soaked and getting more so by the second. At every tiny break from the crazy fits of pressure-washing, I frantically tried to gain control, wildly punching every "surely this closes the sunroof" button. Still nothing. I tried to figure out some way to initiate an emergency stop to get out of the car wash, but the giant, swirling brush outside each car door clued me in. There was no stopping. And there was no way to regain control. I was a prisoner. Oh yes, I would be getting this car wash. I don't even mean my car. I mean me.

Water and suds gushed down my back, even into my pants. In a matter of a few minutes I was riding in an SUV-sized dunk tank.

Don't even get me started on the hot wax. I was so relieved when I spotted the dryer up ahead. What were the chances that thing could dry the inside of the car as it was drying the outside? At least dry it a little. There was hope, anyway. Until I realized that the jet-engine-sized blow dryer blasted all the water still on the roof of the car back through the open sunroof.

Open Heart

My need to control. My rigid, "I totally got this" attitude. I so often hide this concept in my spirit. Instead of trusting God's plan, I try to fix. Instead of settling back to enjoy what could turn out to be His peaceful ride, I panic and squirm and wildly punch the wrong buttons in an effort to put myself on my own track.

Trusting the Lord to orchestrate my life His way, and in His perfect timing, has always been challenging for me. The second there's a little drizzle, my natural response is to immediately shift into "How can I fix this?" mode.

My home-life had some malfunction when I was growing up. It instilled a false idea in me that if I couldn't control that area of life,

I should try all the harder to command and direct order into other parts. "I totally got this." It was a negative thinking pattern and a faithless and ineffective remedy.

God desires that I replace my familiar effort to control with much healthier belief and trust. "Therefore, if anyone is in Christ, the new creation has come: The old has gone, the new is here" (2 Corinthians 5:17 NIV). He wants to reclaim and make new. So not only do my old ways of coping need to be exchanged for new faith, need to be changed by reading God's Word, and need to be replaced with a heart that desires to do His will, but my whole heart needs to grow to trust Him more as sovereign. I need to keep my thoughts open to this concept: God has made me a brand new creation. And this new creation doesn't need to be in charge.

Open to Trust

If I look ahead with restless questions about my future—or my children's or my family's—and then slip into my default need to control, I end up making a big, soggy mess. Giving over control to a sovereign God who is also a faithful and loving God—well, that just makes sense. He's totally got this. Upside, sideways, underside— from every direction from eternity past to eternity future.

"But the lovingkindness of the Lord is from everlasting to everlasting on those who [reverently] fear Him, and His righteousness to children's children, to those who honor and keep His covenant, and remember to do His commandments [imprinting His word on their hearts]. The Lord has established His throne in the heavens, and His sovereignty rules over all [the universe]" (Psalm 103:17-19 AMP).

"His sovereignty rules." Even when life is painful or soggy or topsy-turvy. We can trust His love and we can trust in His perfect plan, no matter what.

It doesn't come naturally for us to let someone else—even God—have control of the renovation our hearts need. Not naturally. But when we relax into the trustworthiness of His control, the path to our future is wide open.

Letting go of the steering wheel and peacefully gliding along in trust is certainly a less stressful way to live. I'm thankful to the sovereign God of love and peace who graciously hangs in there, teaching this fix-her-upper to keep on learning to let go of that need to control. And I'm thankful there is still grace for every big, bizarre incident.

On a smaller scale, I'm also thankful for guys at the car wash who hand you towels when you come out of the car wash. Even though they've been scrubbing dirty hubcaps with those same towels all day. And even if they have to recover first from their out-of-control, hysterical laughter.

Added Accents of Colorful Hope from Rhonda

Speaking of "out of control" (and also speaking of hysterical laughter), what I wouldn't have given to have seen Beth's hair after that kind of wash and blow-dry. Or would it be considered a wash and wax? Just another reminder that real, honest-to-goodness, complete control belongs ever and only to our sovereign Lord. In the list of synonyms for "sovereign," we see words like "supreme," "absolute," "unlimited," "total," "unconditional" and "boundless." It's easy to get behind a God who so completely embodies all these things and more. I'm in. Boundlessly!

Fix Our Eyes on Him

> "That people may know, from the rising of the sun and from the west, that there is none besides me; I am the Lord, and there is no other. I form the light and create darkness, I make well-being and create calamity, I am the Lord, who does all these things" (Isaiah 45:6-7).

Bringing It Home:

Read 2 Corinthians 5:17 again. If you haven't already, commit it to memory. Though He makes our spirits completely new at salvation, are there parts of your lifestyle—habits or hindrances—that you still sense a need for some renewing? What can you do, even today, to help that process along?

This concept of "let go and let God" is not a new one. But it is as important as it's every been. God wants to replace our fallacies with His precepts. Are there any old ways of coping that keep you from more complete trust in God's perfect plan?

Looking to God today to handle our tomorrow takes the pressure off our need to fix and control. List three verses that confirm the promise that God is worthy of your trust.

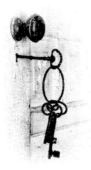

Chapter Twenty-Six

Flooring, Sticking, Inking

Rhonda

"Ya know, we've had that same flooring in the guest bathroom for a long time anyway, right?"

My husband gets a look of fear and dread when I start a conversation like that. But that morning I had been picking up towels in the guest bath when—and this worried me—the towels refused me. I could *not* pick them up! I tugged. They tugged back.

I put real muscle into it and finally won the tug of war. That's when I found that someone had knocked over one of the girls' jars of leg wax. The stuff looked like peanut butter, but oh my, it so wasn't. It must've spilled onto the floor at some point of semi-liquidity, just hidden enough by the bathroom cabinet to get lost under those two towels. That consistency of semi-liquidity in leg wax lasts around .03 seconds. So by the time I found the mess a couple of days later, we were looking at a serious…um…"waxident." The towels were ridiculously glued to the wax and the wax was even more ridiculously glued to the floor.

I was quick to tell my husband that whatever tool he used to get the wax up, he'd better be ready to kiss it goodbye. Because there's some weird science involved in leg wax. Whatever it takes to give a gal smooth legs will also keep shields intact through a rocket's atmospheric reentry. Does. Not. Come. Off. Of anything. And while I was quick to tell him about his tools, I guess I wasn't quick enough. I found his putty knife in the trash later. Bye-bye, putty knife.

It's Our Story and We're Sticking to It

There's a life-giving message that Jesus-followers are called to adhere to—in the stickiest way. Paul said, "Let your speech always be gracious, seasoned with salt, so that you may know how you ought to answer each person" (Colossians 4:6). My personal goal? To be extra salty, extra sticky. Sounds a bit peanut-buttery. And while that's delish, that's not even nearly what I'm after. My goal is to speak words of grace—so full of Jesus and so packed full of flavor that those words make outsiders thirsty for Him. The verse right before it instructs us, "Walk in wisdom toward outsiders, making the best use of the time" (Colossians 4:5).

So how can we walk in wisdom and make the best use of our time here? Backing up another couple of verses gives us a great rundown: "Continue steadfastly in prayer, being watchful in it with thanksgiving. At the same time, pray also for us, that God may open to us a door for the word, to declare the mystery of Christ, on account of which I am in prison—that I may make it clear, which is how I ought to speak" (Colossians 4:2-4). Praying faithfully and thankfully, asking and watching for open doors to share His Gospel—making that Gospel clear. If we want to follow Paul's example, that's exactly how we ought to speak.

The Greek word for "ought" here is *dei*, implying "gluing together." This Gospel message is so vital—so very binding—that it should stick on our every word. Talk about waxing eloquent!

Oh how I want to be quick to tell. May His Gospel be beautifully—even ridiculously—glued to my speech. The clear Gospel. The complete Gospel. The whole ball of wax.

Making Every Word Stick

The sticky-word concept has stuck with me. And not just because it sounds awesome and I'm a word person, though I really am a word person. A quirky, quirky word person.

For instance, I'm not really a tattoo kind of gal. Sorry. But if I ever did get one, I'd want a ballerina skirt. One around each upper arm. And I would want them entirely for the satisfaction of going in and asking for "two tutu tattoos."

Quirky or not, that kind of wordplay has always cracked me up. What's better than a weird tongue-tickler? I thought of that tattoo thing shortly after my sister offered my brother some of her burger and he answered, "No thanks. But I'll take a tater tot or two."

If only dinner that night had been fresh fried fish with French fries. We could serve it with those pickled peppers that Peter Piper picked. Maybe fried up in some of Betty Botta's batter. But only if she resolved that bitter butter bother.

Words are funny little rascals. Entertaining. Incredibly useful. Even though they can get a little tricky—not just sticky. Paul gave us an interesting take on them in 2 Corinthians 3:1-4. "Are we beginning to commend ourselves again? Or do we need, like some, letters of recommendation to you or from you? You yourselves are our letter, written on our hearts, recognized and read by everyone. It is clear that you are Christ's letter, produced by us, not written with ink but with the Spirit of the living God—not on stone tablets but on tablets that are hearts of flesh" (HCSB).

Sticks and Stones–and Other Things That Hurt

Some people in Corinth had been spreading all the wrong kinds of words about Paul. False teachers spreading lies. Talk about twisted. It was like a lie-twister threatening to destroy his ministry. *Word-nado.* But Paul knew his ministry was verified in the lives of the people. Lives that had been changed by Jesus—they were his credentials. Living, moving credentials. We're not talking about wearing just any old ink here. It was a message written on hearts by the very Spirit of the living God.

We do bear His words, allowing the world to read the message He's written on our hearts. Not just sticky, but we ourselves are inky. May we be ever legible!

O Lord, may the world read the message You've engraved on my heart. Your clear Gospel. Untwisted. Unmistakable. May it show up in how I walk, talk, live, love. Make my life the easy-to-read version. By Your power, I pray You'll keep my own words from creeping into that message. Lord, let people read YOU in me, and not me.

The second we stop relying on the Spirit of the Living God to be our message, our flesh is ready, waiting, and all too willing to take over. We can cloud the true message with our own ink, in a manner of speaking. And it's not a pretty picture.

It would be even more disastrous than a homeowner doodling on the interior designer's plans during a reno project.

Let's let the living message...*live.* "Let the spoken word of Christ have its home within you, dwelling in your heart and mind—permeating every aspect of your being" (Colossians 3:16 AMP).

God calls us to leave a mark everywhere we go. Home, work, in the neighborhood—around the globe. Living life empowered by the Spirit of God, depending on Christ to use us to minister to people in a way that changes them—that really will leave a mark. A permanent one.

So maybe I'm not so stuck to my old way of ink-thinking—maybe I'm a tad more tattoo-minded than I thought. I'm...floored.

Added Accents of Colorful Hope from Beth

Thank You, Lord. Thank You for the permanent promise of love. Once we are Your children, no amount of pressure or pulling, stress or struggle, can remove us from Your steadfast devotion. May we walk in the wisdom of Your truth and adhere to Your precepts. Let our speech be evidence of You in our lives, inviting others to know You more. Your Holy Spirit unlocks the boldness we need to be quick to show and even quicker to tell. Help us be a living message of Your work inside us, and when we falter, let our lives demonstrate a living message of Your grace. Amen.

Fix Our Eyes on Him

"Keep your behavior excellent among the unsaved Gentiles, conduct yourself honorably, with graciousness and integrity, so that for whatever reason they may slander you as evildoers, yet by observing your good deeds they may instead come to glorify God in the day of visitation when He looks upon them with mercy" (1 Peter 2:12 AMP).

Bringing It Home

Here's a great verse to memorize: "Let your speech always be gracious, seasoned with salt, so that you may know how you ought to answer each person" (Colossians 4:6). It charges us at every reading to keep words of grace as our goal—words so full of Jesus they cause people to thirst for Him.

Will you pray for sticky/salty/inky words, as we're instructed to in Colossians 4:2-4, and ask the Lord right now to give you an open door to declare the mystery of Christ?

Have you seen people come to faith in Christ or grow in Him because of what the Lord has done in you? Celebrate that blessing! Those changed lives are your credentials. They verify that Jesus is living and working in you.

Will you also pray right now that the Lord will continue to make His message legible in you? Pray for people He brings to mind who need to know of His grace. What can you do to invite them to read His message in your life even this week?

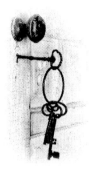

Chapter Twenty-Seven

The Real Reveal

Beth

Three minutes after I finished Gary Chapman's book, *The Five Love Languages of Teenagers* (Northfield Publishing, 2000, 2016), I sat down at the kitchen table with my 13-year-old son while he was eating cereal. Some encounters are simply divine by design. You can bet I've learned that a mom has to ease into some of those profound moments of conversation. I knew I had to be careful not to reveal too much excitement over the hope of some great communicating between us. Ease in. Since timing is everything in cases like this, while Josh chewed Cap'n Crunch, I tossed a few pieces of the cereal in the air to try and catch in my mouth. They all landed on the floor. Still. I was proving I was super-chill.

"Hey, Josh, I just read a book about communicating love to your children. It was about our love languages. What words or actions say 'I love you' the most to you?"

Josh stared back blankly. Then, "Uh…'I love you'?"

"Yeah, buddy. Well, what makes you feel loved—besides the actual words? Maybe, words of affirmation? Like when we point out that you've pitched well, or when we praise you for a good grade in school?"

Josh's eyes were fixed on the back of the cereal box. "Mom?"

I leaned in close for the ooh and the ahh moment—the revelation. "Yes, honey?"

"Which land animal is the loudest—a howler monkey, a hyena, or an African elephant?" The question was punctuated with milk-slurps. Then silence.

Silence Isn't Always All That Golden

Sigh. I hated to let a little silence, a few random slurps, and an African elephant sit between me and the depths of my son's psyche. I tried again, "Josh, what do you think speaks the most love to you?"

"Aahh, Mo-o-o-o-m." His words had an air of "leaky-tire-hiss" to them. He'd had enough.

"Well, OK. If I had to guess, I'd say…the hyena. He, he, he."

"Nah, Mom. I bet it's the African elephant. Can you look at the bottom of the box and find out?" Josh slid his stool back and bolted up the steps to get ready for school.

I ask you, how is a mom supposed to speak love lingo to her son when his mind seems to be off on safari? I suppose I could slather on the SPF 100 and head there with him. Most of us parents will do anything to make sure our child understands this absolute message: You are loved.

True, teaching our kids the art of intentional conversation is great, but deliberate conversation with God is even greater. It's the ultimate conversation skill. Talking with God is like being on a journey—an amazing expedition. The Bible is God's living breath. Part of the conversation. We've looked at the following passage a couple of times, but I don't think we can overemphasize the truths here. Let's look at it in the Amplified version this time. Paul divulges a little of what we can expect if we will but lean in and listen:

> "And how from childhood you have known the sacred writings (Hebrew Scriptures) which are able to give you the wisdom that leads to salvation through faith which is in Christ Jesus [surrendering your entire self to Him and having absolute confidence in His wisdom, power and goodness]. All Scripture is God-breathed [given by divine inspiration] and is profitable for instruction, for conviction

[of sin], for correction [of error and restoration to obedience], for training in righteousness [learning to live in conformity to God's will, both publicly and privately—behaving honorably with personal integrity and moral courage]" (2 Timothy 3:15-16 AMP).

O That I Would Listen Better

Sadly, I don't always have an attentive ear to God or His words for me. I'm sometimes no different than my son is with me. On any given day, my thoughts may be exploring other continents while sifting through struggles, or even wondering if I took the wet clothes out of the dryer. So much inner disruption. Sometimes even while driving. I have to stop and think, "Did I just miss my road?" If I'm not listening to noise on the inside, I'm looking at all things shiny on the outside. All these disturbances can be a "blank stare" to a God who longs to reveal Himself.

How can I know what God has to tell me, unless I am an active participant? I want to be engaged with God. I long to be present in His presence. While I'm working. While I'm in prayer. Even while I'm driving. Focused prayer and Scripture invite His sweet revelation into our lives. Psalms 19:7 says, "The law of the Lord is perfect, reviving the soul; the testimony of the Lord is sure, making wise the simple." Who doesn't need a little revival? A whole lot of revival even. Big reveal right here, friends! The last part of the verse, "making wise the simple,"—I really think I hear God speaking to *me*. Ahh, fellowship.

Before I go any further, I simply can't ignore the African elephant in the room. Timing is everything in cases like this. We don't have as much time today as we did yesterday. No surprise here, but having those honest conversations with God is urgent. He wants to speak to us today, because He has a loving plan for our tomorrow. When I read Scripture, it reiterates God's absolute message to me: You are loved.

"But now thus says the Lord, He who created you, O Jacob, He who formed you, O Israel: 'Fear not, for I have redeemed you; I have called you by name, you are mine'" (Isaiah 43:1).

What a good Father. He appeals to the parent in us, then He speaks to the child in us. We were formed by Him. Redeemed by Him. Reclaimed by Him and for Him! We don't have to look any further to be amazed. "He came to His own, and his own people did not receive Him. But to all who did receive Him, who believed in His name, he gave the right to become children of God, who were born, not of blood nor of will of the flesh nor of the will of man, but of God." (John 1:11-13). He is the ooh and the ahh.

Our Conclusion/Beginning

While writing this chapter, I felt such a desperate pull from God to ask my friend, Meghan Strine, to pray for you in the conclusion. Meghan's story is one of serious, beautiful renovation. Her profound conversation with God on these pages is not a conclusion, but a beginning. The beginning of God's absolute message and real reveal to us all: We are loved!

Father, You met me in a place of deep sorrow and need. And You loved me. It's weird to say I'm grateful for the cancer I had. I am. I'm more amazed by Your mercy. Looking back, how many people, if they knew they were going to lose a parent, would give anything to be able to spend extra time with them? To have those conversations. Deep conversations. Conversations and words that aren't easy to have.

Oh Father, you gave me that sweet time with my mom. My mom and I together, rehearsing the truth about You, and about our faith in You. We rehearsed all those things to each other while she and my dad helped nurse me through my pain, and chemo. All along, my mom and I thought we were rehearsing for me. Then in September of this past year, when You called her home to be with You, Lord, I realized we were rehearsing for her. All those things were true for her, too. Thank You that when we needed You to be real in life's suffering, You were there.

I'm praying for those who read this book. Reveal Yourself to them today, Father. May they be astonished by You. You are real. Help us remember that Your love has nothing to do with how many Jesus books we read, or how much we pray, or even all the ways we try to measure how good we are. It's all about relationship with You. When we are sick. When we are helpless. When we are weary and tired. Especially when we are desperately distracted. You are Lord. May the Holy Spirit confirm this prayer, so these friends will know beyond a doubt that You are the good, good, Father. Amen.

—Meghan Strine 1985-2017

Added Accents of Colorful Hope from Rhonda

I love Meghan's sweet prayer. I'm praying also that yet more conversations are starting up everywhere. Even now.

Lord, lead us to dialogue with You. Make it real. Make it lovely when we need that. And hard when we need that. May it be ever full of You. We always do so need You. Thank You for hearing, listening, caring, answering.

"Then you will call upon me and come and pray to me, and I will hear you" (Jeremiah 29:12).

Fix Our Eyes On Him

"That which we have seen and heard we proclaim also to You, so that you too may have fellowship with us; and indeed our fellowship is with the Father and with His Son Jesus Christ" (1 John 1:3).

Bringing It Home

"Focused prayer and Scripture invite His sweet revelation into our lives." Are you ready to send out an invitation today? The God of the universe waits for conversation with you. Let that soak in. Read Isaiah 43:1 from this chapter again. He calls you "His." How does that change your conversation with Him?

Start up that conversation right now. Consider kicking off your prayer time by singing to Him. Has it been a while since you sang a song of worship to Him? It can be a sweet little contemporary chorus, or a beloved old hymn. Any song that expresses your heart of worship opens up your conversation with the Father in such an intimate way. Encourage your soul to sing even if your voice doesn't. Try this one on for some prayer-worship. Meditate on these thoughts:

Sweet hour of prayer! Sweet hour of prayer!
That calls me from a world of care,
And bids me at my Father's throne
Make all my wants and wishes known.
In seasons of distress and grief,
My soul has often found relief
And oft escaped the tempter's snare
By thy return, sweet hour of prayer!

Sweet hour of prayer! sweet hour of prayer!
The joys I feel, the bliss I share,
Of those whose anxious spirits burn
With strong desires for thy return!
With such I hasten to the place
Where God my Savior shows His face,
And gladly take my station there,
And wait for thee, sweet hour of prayer!

"Sweet Hour of Prayer,"
Words by William Walford, 1845

Chapter Twenty-Eight

A Father/Son Business

Rhonda

It's always a mystery how my DIY projects are going to turn out. The mystery is intense but frankly, not all that fun. Except for the project kind, though, I do love a good mystery. A cozy whodunit? Oh yeah. To me that's positively sensational. I'm even thinking about writing one.

If you're considering writing a mystery, however, it's not always a good idea to make it publicly known that you sometimes sit around thinking of different ways to bump people off. You'd be surprised how many friends can take that the wrong way. I also try to refrain from mentioning that I've now done enough research to successfully dispose of a body without leaving any forensic evidence. It probably shouldn't be a mystery to me why friends might take that the wrong way.

Whatever books I write, there's one mystery that's ever and always in the center of all I hope to communicate. It's the beautiful mystery of our salvation in and through Jesus Christ. "For I want you to know how great a struggle I have for you, for those in Laodicea, and for all who have not seen me in person. I want their hearts to be encouraged and joined together in love, so that they may have all the riches of assured understanding and have the knowledge of God's mystery—Christ" (Colossians 2:1-2 HCSB).

Mysteries–And the Mystery of Christ

Paul struggled with the thought that the new believers in Colossae might swallow some of the lies of false teachers that were springing up. He wanted their hearts to be encouraged with a mystery. Of course, Paul might not have been the best at mystery writing. I mean really, who introduces the mystery, then solves it in the next word?

Then again, I can't blame him for rushing to the exciting conclusion. The solution to the glorious mystery—the one-word mystery that encourages hearts, unites in love, leads to riches of understanding—the word is *Christ*. Mystery solved. And yet at the same time, the mystery continues. It's still mysteriously, miraculously mind-boggling that the Creator of the universe would provide such a gracious and glorious redemption through the sacrificial death of the Son of God on the cross. Oh, the riches of that "assured understanding"! Christ!

The very next words in that Colossians passage testify of the mystery of the hidden treasure that is our Savior. "All the treasure of wisdom and knowledge are hidden in Him" (Colossians 2:3 HCSB). The Father has made known to us in Him everything we need to know to have a right relationship with a holy God. Hidden, but now revealed.

Know what's oh so much better than sitting around thinking of ways to bump people off? Getting on our feet, praying for boldness and thinking of creative ways to love people by sharing this most glorious mystery reveal. Paul said, "Pray also for me, that the message may be given to me when I open my mouth to make known with boldness the mystery of the gospel" (Ephesians 6:19 HCSB).

Publicizing His mystery. It's designed to be more of a "we-dun-it" rather than a "who dun it." And that's truly positively sensational.

Often in do-it-yourself projects or home makeovers, a moment comes when the idea in the mind of the designer or renovator is fully realized. The curtain is pulled back or the cover lifted off or the door opened for the big reveal. Our big reveal is Jesus Christ and the work He's done. Ta da!

The beauty is that the message we have to share is one people can trust. Not because we're necessarily trustworthy people, but because we have a completely trustworthy God.

Trust Issues

I've become convinced that I have a face that people can trust. I have no idea what makes it happen or why they do. I also don't always know what to do with the power.

Sometimes people agree with me without even thinking it through. Surely that shouldn't happen all that often, right? Still, when someone agrees before even fully knowing what I've said, it makes me feel like I'm the "terms and conditions" of people. Click now, read…never. Oh, the power.

I'm letting you know right now, dear reader, that even though you can't see my face, you can trust me most of the time. Okay, you wouldn't want to leave me alone in a room with your nachos for very long. But other than that, trust.

The trustworthiness of a promise always depends on the nature of and the power held by the one making that promise. Let's get real. Once someone adds a layer of melty cheese, if you trusted me, I would question your trust-judgment. But our God? The very essence of who He is in nature is flawlessness. The power He holds can't be compared to anything or anyone else. He has it all.

Paul said in Hebrews 10:22, "Let us draw near with a true heart in full assurance of faith, with our hearts sprinkled clean from an evil conscience and our bodies washed with pure water." Paul is talking to us as believers when he says in the next sentence, "Let us hold fast the confession of our hope without wavering, for he who promised is faithful" (vs. 23).

Love-Trust

It makes sense to have faith in the One who is faithful. It makes sense to trust in the One who is trustworthy. His record is clear. He has never failed to deliver on a promise. Never. God's Word is filled, cover to cover, with one blessed occurrence after another of promises kept.

We have His nature as the basis for our trust in Him. We have His power, knowing He is fully capable of carrying out His promises.

And if that's not enough—which it certainly is—we have His love for us to top it all off. You can trust the One who loves you without limits, without reserve. "But God, being rich in mercy, because of the great love with which he loved us, even when we were dead in our trespasses, made us alive with Christ—by grace you have been saved" (Ephesians 2:4-5).

Our Lord loved us all the way to the cross. His love is perfect. And that leads us to trust Him without the slightest apprehension. Our faith is well-placed. "But You, Lord, are a compassionate and gracious God, slow to anger and rich in faithful love and truth" (Psalm 86:15 HCSB).

David wrote also in Psalm 143:8, "Let me experience Your faithful love in the morning, for I trust in You" (HCSB). Love leads to trust. And trust leads to love. That *is* perfect!

Anytime you encounter a challenge, difficulty, doubt or question, it changes how you see that struggle when you remember that Your Father is trustworthy. Not part of the time. All. In every room. With every heart-adjusting, wallpaper-stripping, another-round-of-sanding project. He is perfect, He is powerful and He loves you with a lavish love. Those are His terms. Those are His conditions. Oh, the power!

The mystery of the Son, the glorious trustworthiness of the Father, the indwelling presence of the Spirit—inspire our love, our faith, our surrender, our dedication to always be about His business.

Added Accents of Colorful Hope from Beth

Lord, Your Word promises that when we draw close to You, the mystery of Your love is revealed. Help us live by faith and not by sight. May we seek to know You more, and allow our toes to hang over the edge of trust.

You know, Father, that we long for safety and security, but that's not Your priority. Your love is zealous and sometimes wild. Your pursuit and jealousy are all for the love of us. We can trust You completely, a God who loves that much. Help us surrender to You and Your perfect plan, in Your precious name, amen.

Fix Our Eyes on Him

"Behold, God is my salvation; I will trust, and will not be afraid; for the Lord God is my strength and my song, and he has become my salvation" (Isaiah 12:2).

Bringing It Home

One more time and just for fun, what is the one-word mystery (Colossians 2:2)? How does knowing the answer to this most important mystery of life change the way we see every other mystery of life, including the questions we have when we're in the middle of a messy life renovation?

This chapter challenges us again to get up, pray for boldness, and think of creative ways to love people by sharing the Gospel. Ready to accept the challenge? A great place to start is exactly where Paul did, asking for prayer. Read Ephesians 6:19 again. Is there someone you've been wanting to share the Good News of Jesus with? Call up a close friend and ask for prayer to do just that.

How glorious that the message we get to share is a trustworthy one! Make a list of all the promises He's made that have been fulfilled. Let it spark a thanksgiving and praise time to the One we can trust in every detail of life—the One we can trust to save.

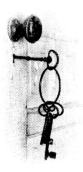

Conclusion

Before and After

Rhonda and Beth

We heard a story not long ago about a woman who had worn herself to a frazzle working on her home renovation. It had been a long, hard process, but Dinah (not her real name) was finally finished! She was getting ready to do some serious woot-wooting. Some of the paint on her new baseboards had gotten scuffed up in the last few reno tasks, though, so she was giving it all its final touchups. She was on the phone with a girlfriend as she painted that last little spot on that last piece of trim. Woot-woot! Dinah raised her glass of iced tea for a pseudo toast to herself and took a big, celebratory drink.

Except it wasn't her iced tea. She had taken a giant swig from her jar of touchup paint. Yuh oh.

While "Chantilly White Number 987" doesn't sound at all tasty, it seems it's not even as tasty as it sounds. Dinah's friend on the other end of the line got to hear her colossal spit-take. It was one impressive *pa-too-ey!*

It's a shame no one keeps records of such things, because Dinah's certainly might've been an award-winning spew. It was solid gold in both distance and density. Great coverage. Ironically, doing her "finish painting" meant she was suddenly not at all finished.

And the Fix-Her-Upper-ing Continues

That's how it is for us spiritually. It doesn't always have to be that frustrating. But it is ongoing. And even though it's ongoing, it doesn't have to feel quite so unfinished. Mostly because of Jesus' finished work of salvation for us on the cross.

Our goal in this life, though, is to become more and more like Christ. In that sense, we never entirely put the lid back on that touchup paint and walk away "finished." We're redeemed gloriously and immediately when we give Jesus our hearts, yes. Our future is forever changed from hell and eternal separation from Him, to living forever in His presence in a place where there will be no sin, no sadness, no suffering.

But even after that most magnificent transformation, the continuing renovation is a lifelong process here on Earth. In this book, we've looked at the truth that, although we no longer have to live under the penalty of sin, our fleshly nature is still part of our makeup and must be battled. We've also been reminded that the Holy Spirit empowers the battle. He inspires and enables this continuing renovation. It's never been about becoming a fix-yourself-upper. It's all about allowing the Lord, who renovates so perfectly, to do a makeover from the inside out.

It's important for us to be reminded regularly that we have a choice. We can choose to lean on Him, trust Him, and invite those inner renovations. Or we can choose to hinder and thwart, squirm, and balk. Some days we choose well. Some days we make a spewy mess. But there is grace for every *pa-too-ey*. And the goal remains to continually move toward becoming more like Jesus.

Romans 12:1-2 has popped up a couple of times through *Fix-Her-Upper*. It's so key—absolutely crucial—for persisting in the glorious renovation process the Lord longs for us to experience. Take a look at those verses in the Amplified version: "Therefore I urge you, brothers and sisters, by the mercies of God, to present your bodies [dedicating all of yourselves, set apart] as a living sacrifice, holy and well-pleasing to God, which is your rational [logical, intelligent] act of worship. And do not be conformed to this world [any longer with its superficial values and customs], but be transformed *and* progressively changed [as you mature spiritually] by the renewing of your mind [focusing on godly values and ethical attitudes], so that you may prove [for yourselves] what the will of God is, that which is good and acceptable and perfect [in His plan and purpose for you]" (AMP).

Before and After-Ever-After

Whether or not the renovation will keep going in each of us will depend on those choices. Will we hinder and squirm? Will we feed our minds on worldly philosophies? Or will we put ourselves on that altar? Will we give Him all? Will we allow our minds to be transformed—renovated, restored, refreshed, refurbished, revived, renewed, and reclaimed—feeding our minds God's truth? At every good choice, one more little corner of our spirit can experience a renovation toward righteousness.

We haven't left out the fact that sometimes renovation is hard. It's dirty and dusty. Sometimes we spew a little paint. There are blisters and sore muscles and sometimes a hammer to a thumb. Sometimes it smarts when God does a renovation work in us. Leaving behind our old ways and our fleshly wants can be difficult and painful and messy. But it's the path to life. Real life. Life the way it's meant to be lived. With joy and peace and purpose built right in.

In a home redo, we all long to see the "before and after," right? It's incredibly gratifying to see the old "ick" become the new "ah."

Spiritually, we've encountered the "before," for sure. We were hopeless in sin and ick. How infinitely more gratifying it is to be completely dazzled at the spiritual "after"—when we see our heavenly Father do a transforming work in our spirit. It's beautiful! Mindboggling! It's over-the-top "ah"! And as glorious as every "after" might be, there's always another. His work in us is ongoing. We get a before and after, and after, and after, ever-after. Woot-wooting evermore!

Our Prayer for You

We're celebrating every single evermore with you! Our friends, it's been our honor to be fix-her-upper projects alongside you through this book. We're also praying that the holy "fixing"—yours and ours—will keep right on going long after this book is closed. It's also our blessing to pray for you. Thank you for being fix-her-upper-ed with us!

O Lord, we thank You for every reader/new friend. We pray for each one. May she experience Your salvation in its most magnificent fullness. May she feel a little less broken even now as a result of digging into the truths in Your Word. Thank You for every time You've used something within these pages to renovate, restore, refresh, refurbish, renew, and reclaim even one of us. There's hardly a more joyous thought, nor grander blessing. We ask that You continue, even multiply, that ministry. And we ask, dear Lord, that You will help us look a little more like You every time we read it. All because of Your love and grace, through the truth of Your Word and by Your renovating power. In Jesus' Name, amen.

About the Authors

Beth Duewel is a writer, speaker, and blogger at fix-her-upper. com. She is a freelance writer for magazines and compilations books and has long been a regular contributor to P31 women's magazine. Beth worked as a recreational therapist and a drug and alcohol counselor for many years. She lives in Ashland, Ohio, where she is happily married to Jerry Duewel. They have three grown children.

Rhonda Rhea is a humor columnist for great magazines such as *HomeLife, Leading Hearts* and many more. She is the author of 11 nonfiction books and also co-authors fiction with her daughter, Kaley Rhea. Their new romantic comedy, *Turtles in the Road*, has just released. Rhonda is a TV personality for Christian Television Network's KNLJ and lives in the St. Louis area with her pastor-hubs, Richie Rhea. They have five grown children and two grandbabies.